The Life and Times of
SUBHASH CHANDRA BOSE

"I am not one of those who forget their past glory in their desire for modernity. We have to make our past our basis. India has its own unique culture which has to be cultivated in definitive streams. We have much to give the world in the form of philosophy, literature, art and science; and the world looks up to us curiously."

—Subhash Chandra Bose

The Life and Times of
SUBHASH CHANDRA BOSE

Praveen Bhalla

Published by
Ocean Books (P) Ltd.
4/19 Asaf Ali Road,
New Delhi-110 002 (INDIA)
e-mail: info@oceanbooks.in

ISBN 978-81-8430-395-7
The Life and Times of
SUBHASH CHANDRA BOSE
by Shri Praveen Bhalla

Edition
2026

Price
₹ 400.00 (Rupees Four Hundred only)

Printed at
R-Tech Offset Printers

Author's Note

"Revolution can transform the mindset of the entire nation. If a nation give up its life force, it would have no right to live. If it continues to live after giving up its life force, its existence would have no value for the mankind."

There is an adage in the ancient Indian scriptures that says: "Great souls are born for the emancipation of people when the earth is inflicted with sins, injustices, immoral acts and exploitation." According to scholars, this statement is tree in all sense. In this context, they cite the instances of ancient religious reformers like Rama, Krishna, Jesus Christ; or popular social personalities like Mahatma Gandhi, Tilak, Bhagat Singh, and the like. In the category of such great people is included the name of Subhash Chandra Bose, the harbinger of Indian revolution. He was courage and sacrifice incarnate; he had initiated a new chapter in the glorious history of India.

Unmoved by the circumstances, illuminated with vigour and spiritual aura, a master of magnetic personality and thoughtful nature – these are the marks of identity of brave Subhash Chandra Bose. He was the only revolutionary who rose into armed rebellion at the national level, and he was the first to do so after 1857. Those who knew him from close quarters, they compared him with a source of energy that could shatter the darkness of despair, prevalent in the people's hearts merely by his presence.

At the initial stage of life, Subhash was influenced by spirituality. He was so profoundly influenced by Vivekananda and Ramakrishna Paramhansa that he gave up everything in search of a Guru, a true teacher. During this excursion, he experienced the truth. Before him came to the fore the pitiable condition of the enslaved India, suffering from the British atrocities, oppressions and exploitations. This was a new turning in his life, now he turned to a new path, and this new path led to the transformation of Raja of Sharda to the Netaji of the world.

Subhash was a true Yogi, a Yogi who had gathered all his vitality to strike at the oppressors. His work was not based on selfish interests, nor did he attach any importance to individual pleasures. He was a Yogi performing the Yajna of Freedom. His selfless service proved a boon to the society and nation.

Subhash Chandra Bose studied the country from a multidimensional perspective. He knew that the country, which was reeling under the curse of slavery for over two centuries, was replete with severe problems like poverty, famine, unemployment, epidemics and natural calamities. Ninety per cent of the population here was illiterate; people were so busy earning their hand-to-mouth existence that they little knew the meaning of freedom. He wanted to introduce a definite project for their development in the society. He emphasized on the abolition of *Zamindari* and princely states and encouraged industrial development and small scale industries.

According to him, caste discrimination and religious narrow mindedness were the obstacles in the path of national integration and unity. He warned that the policy of divide and rule had divided the country into two parts – Hindus and Muslims. If this situation did not improve, the country would have to face the brunt of partition. This was the reason that he made solemn efforts to cultivate cooperation, empathy and harmony among all faiths.

In the context of freedom, Subhash Chandra Bose favoured social, individual, religious and provincial freedom. Together with freedom of India, he also wanted to see the world emancipated from the scourge of imperialism. This great dreamer saw a dream for the independence of the motherland, and he favoured to adopt any means to realize it. He attached significance to non-violent movements. At the same time, he considered revolutionary activities equally useful. He toured different countries of the world and observed the progress of history there, and on its basis he inferred that the use of armed military power was *sine qua non* for freedom from foreign rule. This was the thinking which inclined him towards armed rebellion.

In the viewpoint of Gandhiji, Subhash possessed consciousness and commitment for action. He did not want the essence of freedom, rather he made efforts for complete freedom. He considered Gandhiji's anticipation of change of heart on the part of the British as mere idealistic infirmity. He repeatedly said that no ruler could easily give up his imperialist inclinations and hold; a slave country has to snatch its freedom from the cruel jaws by the use of force.

So far as the structure of free India was concerned, he supported a democratic system which would incorporate the system of socialist and political republic. He wished to see India inclining towards communism which was suffering under the exploitation of capitalists and landlords. He supported the initiation of the youths in politics, so that new politicians and thinkers came to the fore. He wanted to see India transformed into an ideal nation.

If we analyse minutely, we would find that his ideals, doctrines and spirit of devotion towards the nation could not be negated. His personality was so glorious that could not be forgotten over ages. This book reveals every aspect of his life in detail. It is earnestly anticipated that it would be able to satisfy our readers' curiosities.

Contents

1
Historical Cuttack

Cuttack: an important and ancient town in the state of Odisha in India. According to historians, the history of this town dates back to more than a thousand years. This town, which remained the capital of Orissa (now Odisha) for over nine centuries, is still known as a commercial capital of the state. The initial history of Cuttack pertains to Keshri dynasty. It is said that a king called Narupa Keshri, in 989 AD, set up a military cantonment here. Later, this cantonment expanded and transformed into the town of Cuttack. According to the historical evidences, it was King Anangbhim Mahadev, the founder ruler of Ganga dynasty who made Cuttack the capital of Orissa. After the decline of Ganga empire, Orissa came under King Gajapati, a ruler of Surya dynasty. The dignity of Cuttack continued to prevail during his rule too. Mukunddev was the last Hindu ruler of Orissa. After his death, this state changed hands to Muslim rulers, and then to Mughal rulers.

In 1750, when Cuttack passed into the hands of the Marathas, it emerged as a commercial centre. The commercial relations between the Marathas and the English traders of Bengal were established in this very town. Soon, the increasing influence of the English brought Cuttack under their control in 1803.

It was in this historical and ancient town that Barrister Jankinath Bose lived with his family.

Sage's Prediction

It was the month of December in the year 1896. The winter was at its extreme. The town of Cuttack was not untouched by wintry winds, yet the cold season had turned this place quite pleasant. People were busy enjoying winters in many ways. Some people were busy chalking out programmes for an outing, while others were planning for feasts and celebrations. This type of celebration was also being planned in the family of Jankinath Bose. His wife was expectant; it was the eighth month of her pregnancy. According to the tradition, it was the time for performing the custom of *God Bharai* or showering blessings on the expectant mother. This occasion was attended by family friends and relatives.

When the programme concluded, all people returned to their respective places, and Jankinath led his wife to his room and made her comfortable on the bed.

Prabhavati was visibly tired, Jankinath could feel it very well, so he said in an affectionate tone, "You seem to be too tired. Rest awhile."

"It is the time for evening prayers and I have to prepare for that. I shall rest only after that," said Prabhavati rising from the bed.

"There is still time for the evening prayers, so what you should do is to take a rest for some time," saying this Jankinath made her lie down on the bed, and he sat beside her tapping her forehead.

It was just at this hour when they heard a voice at the door, "*Alakh Niranjan*!"

"Who can be there at this hour?" Jankinath looked out of the window.

There was an old sage at the main gate calling for alms, "*Har Har Mahadev*! Will anyone feed this saint?"

Listening to the call, Prabhavati rose from the bed. Jankinath tried to stop her, "Not you, I will go and give something to the saint."

"No one has ever been turned away hungry from this door. I'll go myself to make arrangements for his meals," said Prabhavati as she rose and walked out.

A little later, the holy sage was sitting in the courtyard taking meals. When he had satisfied his hunger, his face glowed in pleasure. He said affectionately, "You have indebted this saint by feeding him. Daughter, I bless that this glory and prosperity may continue with you."

Prabhavati folded her hands and said in a polite voice, "O holy sage! I seek your blessings for a healthy and blissful offspring. I am quite anxious for it."

The saint laughed and said in response, "Daughter, you hold no ordinary being in your womb. He is Lord Shiva incarnate. As Krishna took birth from the womb of Devki and made her a subject of honour, the same way, this offspring would make you and your family immortal in the world. As you are a worldly being, you might feel this incident quite ordinary, but this is the initiation of a new age. This offspring would be uniquely talented who would not be forgotten for ages to come. His actions would culminate into human ideals and ideologies. This is the tempest that would root out all sinners; it will be impossible to check him. So, give up all anxieties, because this being would eradicate the suffering and anxieties of millions of people."

This was the glimpse of the future that the saint painted before her, and then he walked out.

Birth of Subhash

23 January, 1897. Prabhavati was tossing and turning in pain. The elderly women in the family could see the onset of delivery. They knew it well that the time of birth of an infant was round the corner. The nurse asked Jankinath to move out, and then she latched the door from inside.

It took much time. Jankinath stood outside anxiously waiting for auspicious news; however, the baby seemed adamant, he was not inclined to take birth. Maybe he wanted to show to the world that his determination and firmness were going to be the treasure for the country; maybe he knew that the oppressors would scurry for cover when he come into the world, and so he seemed to give a few more wishful moments to such wicked people.

After many efforts, the room reverberated with the cries of the newborn. Lord Krishna had taken birth to take on the sinners. The joy of Jankinath knew no bounds. It was the ninth offspring in his family, he threw open the doors of his treasures and donated open handily to the poor.

Raja of Sharda

Jankinath Bose was blessed with fourteen children, comprising eight sons: Satish Chandra, Sharat Chandra, Suresh Chandra, Sudhir Chandra, Subhash Chandra, Shailesh Chandra and Santosh Chandra; and six daughters: Pramila, Sarala, Tarubala, Malina, Protiva, Kanaklata. Subhash was the ninth child and sixth son of his parents.

A large lively family it was, so it was not possible to pay attention to any one member. Jankinath was busy with his occupation in the court as well as social work. Prabhavati rarely found time from her household duties. Though all children, right from the eldest to the youngest, were showered with infinite affection and care, yet there was a limit to this care in a house with a large number of children. As a consequence, when the child Subhash grew, he became solitary by nature, he suffered from a sense of cowardliness and inferiority complex.

However, there was a woman in the family who shared Subhash's loneliness all the time, she was the maid called Sharda. It was she who looked after all the children in the Bose family. Subhash too was given in her care after his birth. She took care of the newborn right from bathing to feeding. Sharda affectionately called her Raja. She would play with him and say: "My Subhash will become a Raja one day and the world will bow before him."

Knowingly or unknowingly, Sharda was revealing the truth that was bound to take place in the times to come.

□

2
Unforgettable Lineage

The family lineage, with which Subhash was related, had its roots deep in history. According to the available evidence, his family came into recognition from the time of Dasharath Basu. In fact, he is considered to be the founder of Basu dynasty of Mahinagar.

It is believed that Dasharath Basu had settled in Bengal on the invitation of Adisur, the King of Bengal. According to historians, Raja Adisur and Raja Jayant, who ruled from 772-773 AD were the same person. This period is also mentioned as the arrival of Dasharath Basu in Bengal; however, some historians are of the view that he came to Bengal during the rule of Sen dynasty in 1095 AD.

Dasharath Basu had two sons: Krishna and Param. With the passage of time, Param settled in East Bengal, while Krishna Basu continued to live in West Bengal.

From Basu to Bose

The great grandson of Krishna Basu was Mukti Bose, who settled with his family in a village called Mahinagar in south Calcutta (presently Kolkata). The word 'Basu' came to be changed into 'Bose', and gradually, the people of Basu came to be known as Bose.

In the tenth generation of Krishna Basu, there was a Mahipati, who was very intelligent and talented. Impressed by his scholarliness, the then Muslim ruler of Bengal appointed him as the minister of finance and War. Later, he was pleased with his services and efficient governance, and he was honoured with the title of 'Subuddhi Khan'. According to the prevalent royal tradition, Mahipati was also granted an estate as well as a village called Subuddhipur. This place was proximal to Mahinagar.

Of the ten sons of Mahipati, the fourth one was Ishan Khan, he was able and full of positive qualities. He continued to maintain the honour and prestige of his father in the royal court.

Gopinath alias Purandar

Ishan Khan had three sons, who obtained titles from the contemporary ruler. Of these three sons, the second son Gopinath Bose was a master of extraordinary ability and skill. Sultan Hussein Shah (1493-1519 AD) appointed him as the minister of finance and chief of navy. He played a vital role in reforming economy and strengthening the navy. Impressed by his achievement, the royal court awarded him the title of Purandar Khan and rewarded with an estate. This estate, which was located near his parental village Mahinagar, was called Purandarpur.

Gopinath Bose had also dug a one-mile-long pond, called Khan Pukur, in Purandarpur for the use of villagers. The village nearest to Mahinagar was 'Malancha' which was situated in his own garden.

Those days, the Hughli River flew not far from Mahinagar. Therefore, Gopinath sailed on a boat to go to Gaud, the then capital of Bengal. For this purpose, the royal court had granted him a large and magnificent boat. He constituted a strong navy in order to protect the state from any external aggression.

Gopinath left his mark as a social reformer too. According to the prevalent custom of Ballali, the two branches of the Kayastha community did not intermarry. These two branches were Kulin (which comprised Bose, Ghosh and Mitra) and Maulik (which comprised Dutta, De, Roy etc.). Gopinath founded a new tradition. According to him, the eldest son of a Kulin family could marry only within the Kulin community, but the other sons were free to marry in the Maulik community. This tradition, which is usually followed even today, helped to eradicate the familial imbalance of the Kayastha community.

Harnath Bose

Later, the descendants of Gopinath Bose migrated to Kodalia. In his twelfth generation was born Harnath Bose. According to tradition, the Bose family followed Shakta sect, yet Bose adopted the principles of Vaishnava sect. Generally, the followers of the Vaishnava sect are non-violent, so they opposed the custom of sacrifice on the occasion of Annual Durga Puja and stopped this tradition. He is looked upon with admiration for this courageous feat even today.

Harnath Bose had four sons: Jadunath, Kedarnath, Devendranath and Jankinath. When they grew, they set out for different places in search of livelihood. Jadunath was employed in the Imperial Secretariat. He spent most of his life in Shimla. Kedarnath permanently settled in Calcutta. Devendranath was appointed on the post of a Principal and was posted at different places. He too settled in Calcutta after superannuation.

Life Cycle of Jankinath

Jankinath Bose was the thirteenth generation of Gopinath Bose and twenty-sixth generation of Dasharath Basu. He was born on 28 May, 1860. He passed his matriculation from Albert School in Calcutta, and then he studied in St. Xavier's College and General Assembly Institution (later renamed as Scottish Church College), for some time. Then he shifted to Cuttack and completed his graduation from Ravenshaw College. He wished to become a barrister so he returned to Calcutta to obtain his law degree.

While studying, he also worked as a lecturer in Albert College. During this period, he came into contact with important people of the Brahma Samaj: Brahmanand Keshavchandra Sen, Krishnabihari Sen and Umeshchandra Dutta (the Principal of City College). In their company, new ideas got inculcated in him.

In 1885, he settled in Cuttack and started his law practice.

Title of Rai Bahadur

In the year 1901, Jankinath Bose created history by being elected in Cuttack municipality elections. He was the first ever non-government individual to ascend to the post of Chairman of the Municipality. He was appointed the public attorney in the year 1905.

The year 1912 was full to the brim with important, unforgettable achievements so far as Jankinath was concerned. He not only took oath as the legislator of Bengal legislative assembly, but also was honoured with the title of Rai Bahadur by the government.

Despite his being on the government post, Jankinath was full of the spirit of patriotism. He was staunchly against injustice, untruth, oppression and exploitation. He was a public attorney, yet he did not allow this to influence his work. Once the English district magistrate incited him to go with injustice and untruth in a case, but he preferred to resign from his post than to compromise with his ideals. In the same way, he renounced the title of Rai Bahadur in 1930 to protest against the oppressive policies of the British government.

Confluence of Doctrines

After his resignation, Jankinath started working with the local bodies like municipality and district board. He was an active member of educational and social institutions like Victoria School and Cuttack Union Club. He also donated a large sum of money each month, a large part of which was meant to meet educational expenses of the poor students. A large share of his donation went to Orissa, yet his parental village never slipped off his memory. He set up a charity clinic and library in the name of his parents.

Jankinath was a regular participant as an audience in the annual sessions of the Indian National Congress. He was a strong supporter of Swadeshi, however, he never took active part in politics. In 1921, when the Non-cooperation Movement started, he showed his interest in the Congress's Khadi Movement and National Educational Movement too.

He possessed an equal respect for all faiths. He was initiated twice in his life, for Shakta sect and Vaishnav sect. He also chaired the local Theosophical Society. He possessed compassion for the poor people. Prior to his death, he made suitable arrangements for livelihood of his dependants and old servants.

Introduction to Prabhavati

Prabhavati, mother of Subhash Chandra Bose, was born in 1869. Her father, Ganganarayan Dutta, belonged to the Dutta family of Hatkhola (northern part of Calcutta). Dutta family was one of those families that had taken full advantage of the new political order from social and economic viewpoints. This family was known for its riches.

Kashinath Dutta, grandfather of Prabhavati, settled in a small town called Barnagore, which was about six miles from north Calcutta. He gathered a large fortune with his hard work and perseverance. His magnificent mansion was famous far and wide. Kashinath was an educated man. He had worked on an administrative post in M/s Jardine Skinner, a British trading firm. Ganganarayan too was an able and educated person, who followed in his father's footsteps to accumulate further family honour.

Test for Marriage

Eldest among nine brothers and six sisters, Prabhavati was the child on whom the parents doted on. Kashinath and Ganganarayan wished to have a suitable and scholarly bridegroom for her. A number of wealthy families of Calcutta were eager to enter into marital alliance with her, yet Dutta family wished to take a decision patiently. After due thought, Jankinath Bose was finally selected for Prabhavati.

However, it was not an easy task for Jankinath. Before the alliance was settled, Jankinath Bose had to go through a written and intelligence test, which was conducted by Sir Romeshchandra Mitra (son-in-law of Kashinath and the First Indian Chief Justice of Calcutta High Court) and Rai Bahadur Harivallabh Bose (second son-in-law and a prestigious attorney of Orissa). The alliance was approved only after they were fully satisfied.

After marriage, Jankinath settled in Cuttack, and it was how his married life commenced.

□

3
Education

In the year 1902, the child Subhash was five years old. Now Jankinath was worried about his education. He was well aware of his competence, so he wished that he should be properly educated so that he could bring name and fame to the family and lineage. To meet this purpose, it was absolutely essential that proper education was imparted to him.

Those days the British ruled over India, so the missionaries were very active. They had set up a number of missionary schools at different places in order to propagate Christianity as well as create government protégés. However, this also benefited those people who wanted to make their children educated and modern. They could get their children western education through them, and thus helped their wards to link with the world.

Cuttack was a tribal and rural belt, so it was not untouched by the missionaries. A Christian school had been founded there long before, in which most of the students were Anglo-Indians. Besides, Indian children too formed part of students. Subhash's siblings had all been educated in that very missionary school, so Jankinath got him admitted in the same educational institution.

The school was replete with the spirit of western influence with students in western dress and English teachers, and the common language was English in the school. There was no sign of Indian culture and civilisation in the curriculum. When Subhash, born and brought up in Indian tradition, entered the school premises, he felt strange, but then he adapted himself to the surrounding environment and started his study.

Impression of Lawrence

As the school was run by the missionaries, English was the medium of instruction; English also dominated in mutual conversation and interaction. The Hindi-speaking students were caned as a rule. As Subhash belonged to an educated family, he knew some English, but it was not enough for education; it required mastery over the English language; however, he was scared of this language.

Meanwhile, a female teacher named Lawrence was assigned with Subhash's class. She taught English. Despite being a British, she was very soft and tolerant by nature. As compared to other teachers, she was a delicate, compassionate teacher who encouraged students. Her way of teaching was quite different from that of other teachers. She explained each topic in very simple terms, so in no time, she grew popular among all the students. She had special attachment with Subhash, she taught him English grammar very carefully.

The child Subhash was a promising student, he possessed a wonderful ability to understand things. As a result, he excelled in English and other subjects quite easily in which other students struggled. Due to this ability, he became a favourite amongst all.

Bitter Experience

The policy of discrimination was a tool in the hands of the British who implemented it very forcefully. In fact, this was the doctrine on the basis of which the British had succeeded to spread their influence in the country. They made use of this policy in every sector and took complete advantage of it. As Subhash's school was run by the missionaries, the policy of discrimination was at its zenith. During the course of his education here, the child Subhash underwent a number of bitter experiences. He realized the dual mentality and adverse policies right since childhood.

Once he remarked about this situation thus: "A missionary school is a way of implementing the British policies, doctrines, working methodologies and venomous principles. The children in it are inculcated with the seeds of discrimination on the basis of being native and foreign. Something of the sort happened with us too, we were deprived of those rights which were naturally granted to Anglo-Indian children. This can be guessed from the fact that the native children could not sit for scholarship test despite a good showing and attaining the highest position. In addition, native children were deprived of training in horse-riding and shooting, which was regularly available to the British children. I did not pay attention to this aspect in my childhood, yet this went on to torment me in the latter years; my eyes were forced open to this fact. If I should speak my mind, I would say that these incidents filled me with the spirit of patriotism right since childhood."

Subhash attained his education in this missionary school for seven years from 1902 to 1908. During this period, his childlike psyche profoundly observed all aspects – internal and external – of the western way of life. He mastered the Latin language so well that even the English teachers were impressed by his achievement. He was incomparable in other subjects too as his intellectual level excelled over that of others. In spite of all this, his spirit, his mind, his body, his lifestyle, his eating habits – all of them remained untouched by the western culture. He was still infused with Indian culture and traditions.

Admission in Ravenshaw School

After his elementary education, his father admitted him to Ravenshaw Collegiate School in January 1909, when Subhash was twelve years of age. Ravenshaw School had been founded in the year 1868 by Thomas Edward Ravenshaw, the

Commissioner of Orissa, and his wife Mary Symonds Ravenshaw. The curriculum of this school comprised western education as well as Indian culture, history and geography. This was due to the fact that the then ruler of Orissa royal family had donated land for this school and was ever ready to grant aid to this school. In this way, the spirit of Indianness was kept alive in running this school. There was no place for wickedness and discriminatory policies which were prevalent in a missionary school. All students, whether English, Anglo-Indians or Indians, were treated equally; the school rules were commonly applicable to all the students. Moreover, the academic staff was dominated by the people of Indian origin. When Subhash entered this school, he felt as if a new life had been infused into a drooping flower.

□

4
Foundation of Idealism

The school principal, Beni Madhav was delivering his address to the students: "A student should always abide by the ideals of 'learning, service and mutual love'. These should entail the spirit of morality, compassion and selfless service to humanity. The nature distributes all merits and demerits among all people, and does not shower them all on a single person. Thus, it is impossible for any person to have all the merits or demerits. Of course, a person's demerits might be more numerous than his merits, but every person possesses some merit or demerit. Therefore, a person should identify his demerits or negative qualities and cultivate his merits or positive strengths. To achieve this, no place can be better than a school. It is a temple in which the seeds of traits, ethics and mutual fraternity are sown in children."

"Children, you must learn and experience to give up the feelings of 'I' and 'mine', and should embrace the feelings of 'we' and 'ours'; if you did this, envy would automatically be eradicated, and it would cultivate in you sympathetic assimilation of good traits. For children, the foundation of idealism lies in ethics, perseverance and service. A child who abides by these, he thinks, not of himself, but of all other people. He is pained at others' suffering and is enthusiastic at others' joy. He does not hold himself waiting for others to ask him for assistance, rather he is ever ready to help others. He does not speak about 'mine' and 'yours' for the most part, he implements the ideal of 'ours'. He does not accuse others, rather finds excuses to cover up others' shortcomings. He never says that he lacks time, rather he says that he is too busy or weary. He draws everybody to himself, just like a piece of magnet. He illuminates the society like sunrays, he brings joy and bliss on everybody's face."

The words of the principal were sweet, glorious and lively which impressed the students profoundly. Subhash was sitting in the front row and was spellbound in the charm of magical words being stated before him. Each word that the principal uttered found a deep place within his psyche.

"Therefore, children, you must identify your merits, determine your ideals and then propound your idealism. If any one of you has a doubt, he can rise and ask," said the principal concluding his speech.

The assembly was enveloped in silence for some time, and then Subhash rose from his seat and said without any hesitation, "You are motivating to abide by idealism, but I am yet to understand its true form. What do you think is the definition of idealism?"

Beni Madhav smiled mildly at the innocent question and said in an affectionate tone, "According to me, idealism is the fusion of service to others, perseverance and morality. It has no place for hollow ideals, like ego, envy, immorality and selfishness."

Subhash fired his next question, "Why should man follow idealism?"

"Ideals should be followed for the excellence of the soul. The period of childhood, the initial life, is the most adequate for this purpose, because this is the time when a child is initiated into social fold. If Idealism is followed from this time, he will not be affected by social and human demerits lifelong."

"In which form can we embrace Idealism?" Subhash's curiosity was at its peak. Beni Madhav was pleased to the core of his heart on seeing curiosity and intense questioning of the twelve-year-old child. He himself wanted that children should pose questions and assimilate the essence of his statement. However, no other student had come forward, so he was all the more affectionate towards Subhash.

To respond to the question, he guided after thinking for a while, "As I have mentioned that there are four main pillars of idealism, students ought to follow them. They ought to serve the elderly, parents, society and country; they ought to selflessly help the needy and the helpless; they ought to acquire learning through perseverance, and utilize it in the service of the country and social welfare; they ought to accept ethics fully so that they can build a healthy and strong nation."

The enunciation of idealism in simple terms and its meaning and objectives of mass welfare satisfied Subhash, and he vowed to abide by it lifelong.

Influence of Das Sir

Popularly called by students as Das Sir, Beni Madhav Das was born on 22 November, 1866 at Chatgaon (now in Bangladesh). He was a fine scholar and possessed command over different languages. He did his masters in Philosophy and then started teaching in Chatgaon College. In a few days, he transformed this ordinary college into a modern institution by his hard work and competence. He also taught in government colleges in Dhaka (now in Bangladesh), Cuttack, Krishnanagar and Calcutta. Then he was promoted to the rank of principal and worked in different government schools. When motivated by Keshavchandra Sen, he joined the Brahma Samaj in youth itself, and was connected with the publication of a number of institutional periodicals.

Infused with the qualities of devotion and nationalism, Beni Madhav was known as an ideal teacher. He had also studied Economics and History, besides Philosophy. One of his friends described him in these words: "His administration was neither harsh nor vainglorious. His quiet and impressive conduct influenced the students greatly, including those who were mischievous and *mala fide*."

Subhash Chandra Bose had not been in his company for very long, yet he had been impressed by Das Sir to the extent that he continued to abide by his instruction all his life. In this connection, he wrote: "Sri Das was one of those inspiring personalities for me who have influenced my life positively. Most of the students, blessed with his company, found themselves doing well in life. He worked in our school just for one year, but he continued to guide us during this period. As he was a true follower of spirituality and a true worshipper of patriotism, he infused our hearts with the spirits of dedication and patriotism. He often told us incidents from his personal life in order to motivate us. He was inclined to pass most of his time in the company of students. Speaking clearly, he was worth imitating; he was a teacher, scholar, philosopher and explorer; you will find few of such kind."

This statement was not meant for the sake of it. How impressed Subhash was by him can be ascertained from the fact that he formulated a secret plan to meet Beni Madhav before leaving India.

Spirit for Social Service

Influenced by idealism, the child Subhash was willing to devote himself to social service. Together with a few friends, he formed a team and engaged himself in the service of the helpless. He often fed his tiffin to the hungry children on his way to school; he distributed woollen clothing to the poor people in winters; not only this, he spared a day every week to teach village children.

About this time, cholera broke out in an adjoining village; in no time, the entire village was reeling under its devastating effect. People started to die for want of medical care. Subhash was tormented by this pitiable situation; he rose to the occasion together with his team and villagers; and soon, he commanded the service work of the sick. Describing the pitiable condition of the people there, he says: "Their condition was extremely poor; every house was inflicted by cholera; the disease was eating away lives; there were piles of corpses; the entire village was suffering from dirtiness and starvation; food was hard to get for the hungry children, and they all were compelled to suffer silently."

Subhash gathered the local people and undertook a cleanliness drive; he also sought charity from the rich and arranged for medicine and food for the suffering. It was through joint efforts that the village gradually overcame the scourge of disease.

These types of social works made Subhash popular among the people.

□

5
Spiritual Zenith

"Suhrid, where are you?" a voice filled with wonder came from outside.

The youth sitting on the chair was stirred by the known voice. He put down the book in his hand and ran to the door.

Before he could reach the door, Subhash had already entered. He hugged him tightly and said in a happy tone, "When did you come?" And then he said with a touch of complaint in his voice, "Why didn't you inform me about your arrival? I wouldn't have known about your arrival had I not come here. You are a good friend indeed!"

The youth named Suhrid too tightened his embrace round Subhash and said in all affection, "There is nothing like that, dear friend. I was just about to intimate you, but you..."

Subhash interrupted before he could complete what he wanted to, "It is fine that you have come. Now I will be able to spend some time well."

Suhridchandra was the son of a relative; as they did not differ much in age, they were friendly towards each other. Suhrid was studying in another town and was on leave for a few days. His arrival had filled Subhash with pleasure and joy. The two friends sat together and talked.

All of a sudden, Subhash happened to notice the book on the table, he picked it up and asked, "What book is it?"

This book was, *Swami Vivekananda and His Philosophy*.

Subhash asked in all excitement, "Where did you find this book?"

"Our college library has several books on Swamiji; I go there and read them whenever I find some time."

"Did you find this book meaningful?"

"I have never read such a fine book earlier. It describes in detail philosophy and ideals of Swamiji. In my view, you must read it."

Beni Madhav often spoke about Swami Vivekananda, so he knew much about Swamiji. He was a well-known spiritual Guru, philosopher and Yogi. He had breathed his last in 1902, however, his fame continued to rule the country and abroad.

For the past few days, Subhash had an ambition to read his philosophy, and this statement from Suhrid had as if realized his wish. He asked curiously, "Can you lend me this book?"

"Sure, you can take it for sure. I am confident that this book will incorporate novelty in your life and views."

Subhash's joy knew no bounds. He carried this book home and started to read it in all attention.

Influence of Vivekananda

The book pertained to the philosophy and views of Swami Vivekananda. According to him, "The utmost essence of Hinduism has been delineated in Vedanta philosophy, as based on the explanation of Adi Shankaracharya. According to Vedanta, each soul permeates with a part of Supreme Being or Brahman. The goal determined to manifest this divinity is controlled by internal and external nature. This can be attained by action, mental control or philosophy, any one of these or all of them together, in order to realize emancipation. This is the mean sense of all faiths, ideologies, performances, temples, books and literatures. Education is the manifestation of perfection while religion is the manifestation of divinity in man."

Turning over leaf after leaf, Subhash was assimilating the essence of religion.

Vivekananda learnt from his Guru, Ramakrishna Paramhansa a vital fact; that was: 'Being is Shiv.' That means that every being possesses divinity. This became a mantra for him, and he laid down the concept of service to God through service to the poor and the helpless. Until there is even a single man without food, my duty will focus on begetting him food; anything else will be devoid of religion in my view. "O man, arise, awake and stop not till the goal is reached. Keep in mind that service to man is the service to God." This statement formed the basis of his religious and social duties.

Subhash was lost in contemplation. In just one statement, Swamiji had explained devotion to God in a meaningful and logical manner. No doubt, the path leading to realization of God goes through love, compassion, well-being and service to humanity. This sense has been expressed by many other religious scriptures and treatises that God resides in every particle in the Universe, and the only means to attain Him is to serve humanity.

Clouded by his thoughts, he shook his head and started reading the book further.

Swami Vivekananda belonged to that branch of Vedanta that believed in the assumption that no man could be really emancipated so long he lives in the material world. According to him, the duty of an intellectual lies in serving others without any personal greed and ambition. This is the reason that he founded the Ramakrishna Monastery and Mission for serving others. He advised his followers to be pure, selfless and devoted. At the same time, he taught them to adopt Brahmacharya or celibacy. According to him, Brahmacharya could be controlled by physical and mental faculties and continuous practice. He never supported the emerging concepts of astrology and para psychological methods. According to him, these accrued no help in spiritual progress, rather he considered them obstacles in the spiritual path.

Subhash read through the book in a few days. It attained him unprecedented benefit; now he knew the objective and goals of life in true sense.

Title of *Sanyasi*

Extremely influenced by Ramakrishna Paramhansa and Swami Vivekananda, Subhash accepted them as his role models. He now started to lead his life in consonance with their teachings. He was not at all indulged in modernity and luxury, how he assimilated the principle of, 'Simple Living and High Thinking'. The essence of his life now revolved round simple clothing, others' welfare and spiritual thinking.

Brahmacharya or celibacy was an issue which was given utmost importance by Swami Vivekananda; he favoured self-control for this. He said, "Sexual urge is a part of human life; this energy, as bestowed by nature, is very powerful; and if an individual is able to control this source of energy, he becomes divine and frees himself from the worldly cycle. However, it is no simple task to control it. In case this is not excreted, this energy finds a path to excrete by itself; which is mainly due to deformity of physical and mental faculties. Therefore, the internal energy of man should be focussed on controlling it, for which Yoga is the sure shot method. Yoga helps to control sexual energy for its use in a positive manner."

Subhash was in full agreement with the views of Swamiji, so he adopted Yoga as part of his daily life. Now it formed a part of his routine, morning and evening.

As a consequence, now he found himself secluded from the outer world, and started to concentrate himself within self. His activities resembled those of a *Sanyasi*; its impact began to find manifestation on his body, living and thinking too. This was the reason that friends and relatives started to call him *Sanyasi*; however, Subhash never felt bad of this. Due to his spiritual zenith, he had fallen apart from criticism and admiration.

□

6
Renunciation of Home

Having read Vivekananda's views and philosophy, Subhash was now infused with a spirit of *Vairagya* or detachment. He found little interest in worldly affection, activities, selfish actions, family and friends; now his mind and soul were permeated with the spirit of social service, spiritual thinking and Yoga practice; and nothing else. Now, he spent most of his time helping others or meditation. It had immense effect on his studies. Though he was still a regular school-going student, yet he found his studies meaningful. The more he read about spirituality, the more he became detached.

Having studied Swami Vivekananda deeply, he also came to know about his teacher, Ramakrishna Paramhansa. He thought, "Narendra could not have transformed into Vivekananda without Paramhansa. It is truly believed that you can't find the goal without a Guru; because a learned Guru alone is capable to make the disciple realize truth. Therefore, I must set out in search of a competent Guru."

His desire to have a Guru became so ardent that he left home without telling anything to anybody. He set out to different places of pilgrimage in search for a capable Guru.

Realization of Truth

Touring from one holy place to another, Subhash travelled for many days. During this period, he contacted a large number of sages, saints, *rishis* and priests; he lived in their company for many days, but he did not find any of them who could become his Guru: Some of them taught to neglect others' faiths, while others wanted to grind their own axe under the garb of selfish motives: Some of them had taken to this path just to exploit people; while still others had ambitions to attain the supreme powers. He found that those who claimed detachment were themselves deep in the marsh of worldly matters.

Looking at this reality, Subhash lost his faith in them. In this connection, he once said to one of his friends: "I found all the saints and sages deceptive; they claimed detachment, but still seemed mired in worldly illusion; their garb was just to create illusion about them; they had chosen that path for satisfaction of their selfish ends and desire for wealth."

Subhash knew well that a great Guru like Paramhansa took birth only as an exception. Therefore, he gave up his endeavour to search a Guru like him, and thought it fit to follow his teachings like Ekalavya had done.

With this, Subhash put all this behind him and returned home.

Tale of Slavery

During his pilgrimage, Subhash failed to find any learned Guru, but this gave him an opportunity to know and understand the real situation of India. During this period, he studied the pitiable condition of the Indian society. He found people struggling in poverty, starvation, penury and existence, and he was moved by this situation. People did not have means to earn livelihood, leave alone the basic amenities of life. And the English policies were like rubbing salt onto the wounds. The English officers treated the common people like slaves. The English dominated the government high posts, while the Indians were appointed on petty and household jobs in the households of the English irrespective of their competence. The Indians were prohibited for entry into gardens and selected roads, and those who violated this, were caned mercilessly. Besides, they were discriminated against in public conveniences.

This situation was not limited to towns alone, even the farmers and craftsmen living in rural areas had to face such a situation. They were taxed heavily and exploited, while they were given no facilities regarding cleanliness, hygiene and medical services. Government aid remained negligible even during famines or droughts.

Subhash had seen discrimination, exploitation and oppression at government hands for the first time. Until this time, his sentiments were limited to spirituality and social service; he was ignorant of the poor condition of the prevailing Indian society, as he was of the view that the English were efficient and able rulers. But only now he realized that the Indians were slaves in their own country. He had never imagined such a miserable condition; now his illusion had been torn apart; now he nursed feelings of rebellion against injustice and atrocities.

Subhash was not yet influenced by revolutionary ideas, yet the future Subhash was now beginning to take form within him now. In this context, he once said: "If you wish to know the people from close quarters, touring remains the best means for this. I have perceived this fact myself when I was looking for a spiritual teacher. That period of time was the most troublesome for me, not physically but mentally, because I came to know of the truth of an enslaved life. An unseen aspect of life had become manifested before me, and now I could see a vague future before me."

□

7

Political Upheaval

For two centuries from 1747 to 1947, India had been mercilessly crushed under the insulting, oppressive and exploitative slavery. At this time, the world was progressing rapidly, while the British were busy exploiting India economically while aiming to destroy the social fabric too. They crushed the people's sentiments, needs and rights by oppressive policies.

The law of nature says that, 'Excessive pressure results into explosion'. This pressure at the British hands became unbearable, and as a consequence, the volcano of people's anger erupted. The revolution of 1857 was the expression of this flame which was ready to destroy the English rule. The English had succeeded to suppress this historical revolution with their diplomacy and power, yet it resulted into raging of anti-British sentiments. This opposition was not limited only to a few places, rather it spread to different places all over India.

Until now, the Indian people felt helpless and hapless before the oppressive policies and exploitation, yet with the emergence of leadership in the form of freedom fighters and revolutionaries, they came together to oppose the British tooth and nail. This flare comprised people from all walks. People kept aside all their differences on grounds of castes, faiths, untouchability, prosperity, sex, education, and they all came together to attain freedom.

The situation was turning volatile with every passing day. The mass movement was spreading rapidly, and it was sufficient to make the British worried. Now it appeared as if the end of imperialism was fast approaching. In such a situation, the British officials adopted wily policies. As the movement comprised mainly two communities: Hindus and Muslims, they decided and worked to sow the seeds of animosity between them, and thus paved the way for the disunity of the country.

At that time, Bengal was a province in which both Hindus and Muslims lived in equal numbers. To carry out their plan, the government partitioned Bengal; it was said that it was being done for administrative convenience; but in fact, it was meant to sow the seeds of separation between Hindus and Muslims; and they aimed to use this tactic to strengthen their position in India.

Finally, Lord Curzon carried out the partition of Bengal under his policy of 'Divide and Rule'. This was the policy which the British used to their greatest advantage. Actually, they had started to use this policy right since their arrival in India. They had used this policy to reduce the influence of the French and Portuguese traders in India, when they played Indian rulers against one another with a view to weaken them. As a result, almost the whole of India fell under their dominance. We can see this policy as the greatest weapon in their arsenal, before which the opponents were crushed; however, this time, their trick did not go well.

Wave of Opposition

The partition of Bengal was a terrible hurt; it had hurt the innate sentiments of every citizen in the country. It angered people like never before. They could see the wickedness of the British people. In no time, entire India erupted to oppose the partition; protests were held, demonstrations were taken out, mass meetings were held, slogans were raised against the government. This type of movement was started in the Punjab, where Lala Lajpat Rai led the movement. He was popular among his colleagues and common people as Punjab Kesari. As a result of his efforts, the movement spread to the whole of Punjab including Ferozepur, Rawalpindi, Sialkot, Lyallpur and other places.

The objective that the British had in mind while partitioning Bengal had been rendered a failed plan by Hindu-Muslim unity. This partition could not part their unity, love and brotherhood; rather it brought them closer still, and now people were set against the wicked British policy even more vociferously. The government set aside all policies, and made use of cruel repression. It formulated a law to ban all demonstrations connected with the movement. The situation became so volatile that even peaceful demonstrations were heartlessly crushed.

However, the government had to bow down before the protestors. The partition of Bengal was finally struck down in 1911.

Rise of Revolutionaries

The partition of Bengal emerged as the most important event after the rebellion of 1857, because this made the whole of India rise in protest against the British. The part of Indian society, that remained dormant despite all the atrocities, was shaken awake after this unreasonable action of the British. As a result, revolutionaries raised their heads in all parts of India; they believed in responding to the government's policies with bullets and hand grenades. A number of revolutionary organisations were formed and they were mutually linked in a planned manner, and thus they all worked in unison.

The revolutionaries were replete with the spirit of nationalism; they were ready to sacrifice themselves for the country. They were looked with respect throughout the country, except of course the moderates. These revolutionaries were especially popular among the youths, especially students, who were all ready to follow in their footsteps in the path of revolution. This was the reason that we could find the pictures of revolutionaries hung together with those of Gods and Goddesses in the rooms of the young people.

□

8

Seeds of Revolution

Ravenshaw School was not untouched by the wave of nationalism and freedom, mainly due to Beni Madhav Das. He was on a government post, yet his mind and psyche were filled to the brim with the spirit of nationalism. Only the most intimate people knew that he had links with a revolutionary organisation of Calcutta, and he assisted the revolutionaries secretly. Besides, he had taken upon himself the task of inclining the youth towards revolution.

With this aim in view, he held a secret meeting, which was attended by Subhash also. Addressing the meeting, Beni Madhav said: "This is somewhat of an irony that our motherland, despite being the mother of crores of sons, is being crushed under the atrocious foreigners. In the ancient times, India was known as *Devbhumi* (land of Gods), *Tapobhumi* (land of penance) and *Veerbhumi* (land of the courageous), but now it is known as a slave country, as a colony. We blame the English for this, but if we look at this phenomenon objectively, we find that no one else but we ourselves are responsible for all this. The demerits like enmity, envy, disorderliness, lawlessness, comfort, disbelief, deception, selfishness, caste discrimination have disunited us all, due to which the English have succeeded to rule over us. This slavery, penury and exploitation are the outcomes of our delicate nature and lack of foresight. The British went on crushing us, and we followed them in their footsteps like a sagging tree. With time, the situation turned so difficult that we have given up all of our self-pride, self-respect, courage and tolerance; however, some of us today are making a bid to keep aside this timid tolerance and light the flame of revolution. It is our duty that we should sacrifice ourselves in this fire of revolution and make it so intense that the British empire is burnt to ashes in this. It is true that every person cannot become a revolutionary, yet we can certainly assist them in different ways. O young people on whom the future of India rests, take a vow now that you will do everything that is possible in realizing this objective."

The call for revolution kept echoing in the mind of Subhash even after the meeting had closed long before. He somewhat knew of Indian freedom movements, British atrocities and pitiable condition of India under foreign rule. He had many misconceptions about revolution and revolutionaries, but this address by Das Sir had revealed before him the unseen truth. After this, Subhash was excited to know and understand revolutionaries. He took interest in reading literature pertaining to them. In a few days, he was now inclined to reading revolutionary literature in place of religious books; now the pictures of revolutionaries found place on the walls of his room. This transformation was in fact the sowing of the seed of revolution.

Harsh Decision

When Jankinath stepped into Subhash's room, he was amazed. He found the pictures of well-known revolutionaries hung all over the walls in his room; the table was full of revolutionary literature. He could not believe his eyes. He pinched himself to ensure if it was not a dream, but the scenery was not to change. He had entered that room after a long time. He was confident that Subhash was being educated in an English environment, so he could not be influenced by the patriot revolutionaries; yet the truth was contrary to his expectations; Subhash had now taken the path of patriot in his life.

The same moment, his mind resonated with the forecast of the sage who had said: "This is the tempest that would destroy all sinners; it is simply impossible to check him."

He shivered at the thought of some unknown fear, he perspired profusely. He removed all the pictures and collected all books, yet he was unable to find tranquil composure, he was restless.

He acquainted Prabhavati with this fact too, "Are you aware what your lovely son is doing these days?"

"What has he done, why are you so angry with him?"

"He has gone mad with patriotism, his blood was boiling," his voice now expressed a higher level of rage.

The mother protested, "What are you talking? My Subhash could not do so. How do you know this? You have certainly been misinformed."

Jankinath threw the pictures and books before her and said, "Look at all this, I have just removed all this from his room. This is all the consequence of your extreme affection."

When confronted with evidence, Prabhavati grew anxious. She cried, "What will happen now? Do you think that our Subhash…? Is that sage's prediction bound to be true…?"

Jankinath interrupted before she could complete what she had to say, he exclaimed, "No…No! Nothing of the sort will take place. We will have to check him right now, if we don't do this right now, the future may hold trouble for us."

"What will you do?"

"Let me think about this," he said and with this he thought over the matter gravely.

The room fell silent for some time.

Then suddenly, Jankinath breached silence and said, "I have decided what should be done."

Prabhavati looked at him with a massive question mark in her eyes.

"Subhash's education is almost complete now. I'll send him to Calcutta for further studies."

"Send him to Calcutta! What are you saying? I will not let you do this," the affectionate mother cried in the fear of separation.

Jankinath explained to her, "Prabha, this is the only way to reform him. If you want his good, don't impede his progress. It is only a few years when he would be back with us after his studies."

Prabhavati approved with a stream of tears flowing down her cheeks.

The same month, Jankinath made all preparations and got Subhash admitted to Presidency College.

□

9

Town of 'Kali'

About 160 kilometres from the Bay of Bengal, on the bank of Hughli River, is located the ancient and well-known town of India called Calcutta (now Kolkata). This town, connected with the British imperialism, is also called the Gateway to East India. This town is prosperous in terms of education and culture, and reflects a number of historical events in its history.

It is believed that the etymological origin of the name 'Calcutta' is 'Kali', the popular Hindu Goddess. The people here were the devotees of Kali, so this town came to be known as Calcutta. This town finds mention right from the documents of the ancient times to those in the Mughal times and later. Ancient Chinese travellers and Persian traders have mentioned its sea coast as a trade port. We can safely say that this town is one of the earliest towns of modern India.

Calcutta is linked with the renaissance era. In the year 1690, the English traders of the East India Company, had set up their colony here. With time, in 1698, the company bought three villages, and developed them as a town. Following the order of King George II of England, the first civil court was set up here in 1727. The same year, the municipality was set up here and election for the post of Mayor was held.

In 1756, Nawab Siraj-ud-Daula of Bengal attacked the British and brought Calcutta under his command, and it was then named Alipur. However, within a year, the British won it back. In the year 1772, the British government made it the capital of British India, and it retained this status until the year 1912.

Dhoti-panjabi, fish and rice, Bengali *rasgollah*, Calcuttan betel leaf, Durga Puja and Hughli River – all these form the real identity of historical Calcutta. And this town is also known for yet another feature, that is the, 'the proud place of being the birthplace of revolutionaries, patriots, nationalists, poets and literateurs; as well as its supreme contribution in freedom struggle of India'.

Calcutta has the fortune of playing the central role in each stage of the Indian freedom struggle. A great number of institutions took birth here, including the political institutions like Indian National Congress; cultural institutions like Hindu Mela, and revolutionary institutions like *Yugantar* and *Anusheelan*. The list of the great people who took birth here is very long, the names of Swami Vivekananda, Rabindranath Tagore, Bankimchandra Chatterjee, Aurobindo Ghosh, Bipin Chandra Pal, Surendranath Banerjee, Rashbehari Bose, Khudiram Bose, and Chitranjan Das are only a few among those who have and brought glory to this town.

As soon as Subhash stepped on this holy land, his heart jumped in joy. His limbs were excited by the fragrance of the blood of revolutionaries; he felt a sense of belongingness in the atmosphere of this unknown town which was permeated with mutual love and harmony. Looking at the open sky above, Subhash breathed in deep and then he set out towards his objective.

Presidency College

Presidency College was a prestigious college, not only in Calcutta, but in the whole of India. Many well-known revolutionaries, literateurs and poets had been students of this college. Studying here was no little honour for Subhash. As he had been indelibly impressed by Swami Vivekananda and his ideas, he chose philosophy as his subject of study in B.A.

Like Calcutta, Presidency College too has a long history. It was founded by the well-known Raja Ram Mohan Roy on 20 January, 1817. In the beginning, this was known as Hindu College, but after it came under the British, they renamed it as Bengal Presidency College in 1855.

Raja Ram Mohan Roy was influenced by the western educational system, so he set up the college on modern lines. Its curriculum included subjects like Spirituality, Philosophy, Sanskrit and History; together with subjects like Science, Mathematics and English. This helped the students to connect with the Indian culture, while they were able to renounce the fundamental beliefs and evils in order to embrace the path of healthy social and community development.

Presidency College was under government control, but it was the centre of revolutionary ideology; the Indian students of this college supported revolution and often helped the nationalists.

However, Subhash was a different case. He was absorbed in philosophy in isolation from all these; he wanted to pass the examination in the first division.

Influence of Tagore

Subhash, who accepted social service as his creed, was profoundly influenced by the National poet, Rabindranath Tagore. Tagore had been awarded the Nobel Prize for Literature in 1913. With this, he grew popular all over the world. His speeches were held all over the country and abroad; Subhash too heard him a number of times. He had also delivered a speech in Presidency College, which made Subhash his follower.

Admiring him once, Subhash said, "The philosopher Rabindranath Tagore has bestowed upon us novel views on cooperation and progress, these should be taken as invaluable treasure of literature and society. He struck at disintegration of the society, and emphasized on cooperation, welfare and selfless service. In student life, he was very popular among the youths like me, because he presented the essence of our heart in a new form."

Subhash admired Tagore, and the other way round was also equally true. Tagore was so profoundly impressed by the revolutionary views and tasks of Subhash that he dedicated his famous poem *Ekala Chalo* (March Alone) to him.

□

10
Oaten Incident

Most professors in Presidency College were of British origin. Their conduct and nature manifested the dual British policy. This was the reason that they looked down upon Indian students with hatred. Students too knew of this well, but Subhash never paid much attention to them. However, there was a professor in the college who had perplexed even the most tolerant students.

He was Prof. Oaten – fair complexion, brown hair, long moustaches, a stout body, eyes covered in thick glasses. He was called Oaten Sahib by the college staff, but the students called him a dictator. He had been given this name only because of his mentality. He was a staunch supporter of fundamental Christianity and considered Indians no better than slaves. Oaten was snob about his being a British. His ego was so high that he did not shy away from shouting at his co-professors of Indian origin; however, he little realized that a man had entered the college who was about to bring him to his senses.

You Bloody Indian...!

One day, Subhash was returning from the library with some books. As he walked by a classroom, he heard the cries of a student, coupled with scornful scream, "You all Indians are stupid and worthless. Take it granted that it is beyond your capacity. I must have realized that a donkey could never be transformed into man. However hard you may try, you would continue to reel under our feet."

With this, the cries went on abated.

Subhash was stunned to hear all this. Agitated, he peeped into the class. The view inside was horrible. Oaten was caning an Indian student mercilessly, who was bleeding at some places even.

"Beasts like you can be reformed only through this; you can be brought on the path only through this, you bloody Indian...!"

The last three words filled Subhash with flames; they made his blood boil. He entered the classroom and held Oaten's hand and said in a harsh tone, "What are you up to? You cannot hit him."

Oaten was taken unawares for a while, how could anyone dare hold his hand? He had never imagined this. This was a daring act, and he never hoped it. He raged in fury still more, "Let go of my hand! How dare you hold my hand!"

"You must leave this young man and beg sorry for your misconduct," Subhash thundered.

"You have gone mad. Do you know what you are saying? If you want your well-being, just get lost from here," Oaten cried trying to get himself freed.

Self-respect running in the veins of Subhash turned into energy; Oaten could not get his hand freed despite his stout body; it was for the first time that a wolf had confronted a lion. This encouraged the students present there, they all clapped in unison and motivated Subhash.

Oaten's vainglory was shrunken to its proper size, he stuttered throwing his cane, "I'll get you punished for this." He left only after Subhash loosened his grip.

Punishment for Justice

How could Oaten sit silently, he had never borne with such disrespect before. Shattered at this, he wanted to bite like a snake. He went to H.R. James, the Principal and described the entire incident the way he liked. He concluded his statement with these words, "It appears to me that Subhash is connected with revolutionaries. He has dared to behave like this. If this is continued, other students too would stand up against us; therefore, he deserves a severe punishment."

James was out of his wits. He summoned Subhash that very moment and instructed him, "You are a promising student, it does not behove you well to conduct yourself like this. Your conduct with Prof. Oaten is simply unfit and uncivlised; beg sorry of him and keep your focus on your studies and nothing else."

Subhash tried to present his side, "Sir, he was mercilessly caning a student, I only stopped him from doing this; I don't think I was wrong to do this. If you wish..."

James cut him short, "I don't want to listen to anything. You'll have to beg sorry of Prof. Oaten, else I'll take strict action against you."

Prof. Oaten, sitting on a chair in the chamber, swelled up his chest thinking that this staunch guy would have to bow before him; how dare of him! He was smiling to himself.

But he little knew what Subhash was made of, who said in a firm voice, "I don't accept to bow before injustice, there is no question of begging sorry. You can take any action you wish."

"Okay, I suspend you from college for one month," James decided.

Leadership for Strike

By this time, Subhash had become popular among students as a nationalist revolutionary. His courageous action was the talk of the college. It was simply unimaginable for them to think that a student like Subhash, who was always absorbed in his study and spirituality, could ever take such a revolutionary step. The students, who had witnessed the incident themselves, discussed every word and action that occurred in the classroom. Just then, a student came there and declared, "The principal has suspended Subhash for one month."

"What...! How could it be that? It was Prof. Oaten who was at mistake. We'll stand by Subhash. The Principal will have to retract his autocratic order," all students spoke in unison.

With this, the students decided to strike. It was not in the nature of Subhash to bear with any injustice, so he agreed to lead the students.

Triumph of Truth

The strike continued on the third day. Students refused to join classes and started shouting slogans at the main gate of the college. They demanded that the suspension of Subhash should be taken back and Prof. Oaten should beg sorry for his conduct. The college administration was shocked at this, it fined the striking students, but the students remained unrelenting.

Seeing no effect, the administration thought of playing a trick. Under it, some professors threatened while others were allured, in order to secure division among students.

A professor approached Subhash and said, "Are you aware what will be its outcome? The college administration will only expel you for life. The proper thing to do is to stop all this and beg sorry. I assure you of saving you from any punishment."

Subhash looked at the professor for a while and then said confidently, "If our struggle is meant for truth and justice, then we have nothing to fear about, because its outcome will fall in our favour."

"This confidence will spoil your life; it would be better for you to accept my proposal, else you should be ready to face the consequences." With these words the professor departed from there.

However, Subhash did not retract his steps, the strike continued as before.

The students' strike in the famous college became a topic of discussion. The government did not want it to become a nationwide issue, so it interfered and passed an order to settle this issue. As a result, the college administration had to bow down and Prof. Oaten had to beg sorry. Subhash was admonished and his expulsion was retracted too.

On this occasion, Subhash had said, "This victory is not ours, but that of truth and justice. It goes on to prove that God was always on our side throughout this struggle."

A few days passed peacefully when Prof. Oaten once again started to show his colour. He wanted Subhash to commit some mistake, for which he could victimize him and get him expelled from the college. For this, he aimed at those students who had been part of the strike. He started to cane them for no justification, he often insulted them. Subhash could see through his motive, but he had resolved that he would teach Oaten a lesson before he was expelled.

One day, Oaten caned a student heartlessly. Subhash was unhappy at seeing his swollen hands. The revolutionary within him was shaken awake, and he decided to do something about it.

It was two in the afternoon, Subhash stood at some distance from the college. The sun was blazing hot, the roads were scorching in heat, the environment was dry and the atmosphere quiet. But Subhash was not attentive to all this phenomenon, his eyes were fixed towards the college gate.

When a student appointed for this purpose saw Oaten coming out of the gate, he signalled to Subhash, who folded his arms up. When Oaten reached him, he stopped him.

"So, what are you up to? Hiding your face from friends!" Oaten laughed at him.

"I am here to teach you a nice lesson," retorted Subhash.

Oaten knew what was in store for him. He hit before Subhash could strike, and with this, the two grappled. Subhash saved himself and attacked.

Oaten was physically strong, but the rapidness with which Subhash was hitting him made him helpless. In no time, he fell down, while the students hailed Vande Mataram.

Having done this, Subhash moved away from there.

□

11
Expulsion for Life

Soon, Oaten controversy was the talk of the town. A prominent paper depicted this as an act of revolution, while the college administration dismissed it as an incident of indiscipline. The incidence of an Indian student thrashing an English professor was unbearable for the government; therefore, a committee was constituted to inquire into the matter and punish the guilty. This committee was chaired by Sir Ashuthosh Mukherjee, Justice of High Court and Vice-Chancellor of the college.

Having heard both parties and witnesses, the side of Prof. Oaten was proven weak; however, the committee biased against Subhash and decided for a harsh punishment. Under this, he was not only expelled from college, but was also prohibited from taking admission in any educational institution.

Subhash knew that he had been meted out injustice, so he refused to bow before this decision. He took his luggage and left for Cuttack the same day. He had no feeling of guilt, rather his face illuminated with the light of truth.

People thought that his future was now bleak, yet the confident Subhash was looking at this incident as something which could transform his life. He was now fully ready to embrace the future struggle.

Later speaking on his position, he had said: "That day remains a memorable one for me, because my life took a new turning from then onwards. It was the first occasion when I had felt joy after having undergone suffering, the joy was so subtle which left all other things insignificant. At that time, I had to pass through a hard test enveloping principles, ideals, justice, truth and nationalism. Success in that test determined the path of my life."

Waiving of Expulsion

Subhash returned to Cuttack and engaged himself in social work. He toured the adjoining villages and tried to resolve the problems being faced by the villagers. He served the villagers suffering from flood, famine or epidemics. He was still influenced by religious ideals, yet he was not much enthusiastic about spiritual matters and contemplation. In this connection, he quoted Vivekananda, "Absorbed in religion can take you away from social responsibilities and worldly affairs, but you cannot attain God till people around you are tormented with suffering. In such a situation, detachment from the society is like fleeing from social responsibilities and duties. In my view, it is impossible for such a person to attain God. The key to real religion is spirituality and contemplation, together with compassion, others' welfare and selfless service."

Subhash served the society little worried of his future, while Jankinath was much anxious about him. He talked to his eldest son, Sharat Chandra, who had returned from London as a barrister and was doing his legal practice in Calcutta. He talked for Subhash's admission in a number of colleges, but he was clearly informed that he could not be admitted until the expulsion was in force.

He made use of his influence, tried hard, convinced government officials, and then only, his expulsion was waived off.

Strange Conditions

After his expulsion was waived off, Subhash could have taken admission in any college, but the problem remained same as before. Only two colleges in Calcutta, Presidency and Scottish Church, conducted education in Philosophy. It was impossible for him to get admission in Presidency College, so Jankinath contacted Scottish Church College.

"You want Subhash to be admitted in this college, don't you?" the principal looked at him with a lot of questions in his eyes.

"Yes, Sir," Jankinath said briefly.

"I am sorry, this is not possible."

"But why?" Jankinath was astonished at this response. "His expulsion has been waived off, he should be admitted now."

"But the accusation that Subhash was charged with will make no college to admit him," said the Principal.

"It was none of his fault, nor did he hold any untoward intentions. Whatever he did was against injustice."

"We have nothing to do with who was right and who was wrong. In the view of this college, his action was unjustified, so I am unable to admit him."

Jankinath fell silent for a while. A tempest of anxiety rose within him. The principal was not unjustified, the charge on Subhash was serious, and no college could sanction his admission, but then, this could jeopardize his future too. Thinking this, Jankinath emphasized, "Look, he has committed a mistake, but now he is ready to reform. He is a promising student. If you don't help, his competence will be destroyed; therefore, I beseech you to find some way."

The principal thought. It could not be acceptable to him that a student's career should be spoiled. In the end, he said, "You will have to bring a NOC (no objection certificate) from Presidency College Principal."

Jankinath was out of his wits at this condition. He said excitedly, "Why will Presidency College issue such a certificate?"

"Look, this is the only way for Subhash to be admitted here. If you bring this certificate, I would have no objection to his admission," said the principal straight.

"All right, I'll come back to you soon," said Jankinath and rose to walk out.

Final Bid

The condition was strange, as it was next to impossible to bring a certificate from the person who himself had expelled

Subhash; but Jankinath was resolved to help his son. He had taken up a difficult task, so he made to Presidency College. Mr. James had been replaced with the new principal, Mr. Wordsworth.

When Jankinath approached him, he retorted, "Do you know what you are asking for?"

"Yes, of course, I am telling what I mean. I need an NOC from you," Jankinath said coolly.

"Subhash has been expelled, how can an NOC be given to him now?"

"His expulsion has been waived off, now he is free to take admission in any college he wishes, and you cannot refuse this request now."

"This certificate is issued to only competent, obedient and disciplined students. This cannot be given to a student who is adjudged as mischievous and undisciplined. The entire college environment has worsened due to this case. The students no more have a feeling of respect for professors, now they are wont to rebellion at the slightest pretext, and all this happened due to none other but Subhash," Wordsworth shook his head in disapproval.

"Subhash is a talented student, you cannot negate this fact. As far as the matter of indiscipline is concerned, you are well aware what had actually happened. Had the college administration taken a justified decision, such a situation would not have ever arisen. In my view, he has not done anything unjustified," his voice was gradually becoming bitter.

Wordsworth was unnerved at this, still he said, "Whatever arguments you may put forward, but his conduct could not be overlooked, so simply give up all hopes of an NOC."

"All right, I will present this case before the government and then I'll see what makes you hold back the certificate."

The final trick worked. The college had become a subject of scowl in the Oaten case, the criticisms published in newspapers had shaken its prestige, while this case also helped to spread a wave of disaffection against the government. The matter had gone so worse that the government had decided to close down the college itself, this situation was brought under control somehow. The transfer of Mr. James had occurred only due to its repercussion.

Wordsworth did not want to take any risk, he knew that he could be axed if this matter was raised again. Therefore, he said in a hushed tone, "Well, the future is more important than the past, and I am ready to issue this certificate looking at the future of Subhash."

Jankinath grinned within him.

The next day, Subhash was admitted to B.A. third year in Scottish Church College. This incident occurred in the year 1917. Fully detached from spirituality, Subhash found action more appealing than religion. Now, he paid more attention to the political developments occurring in the prevailing times.

Military Training

Right since the beginning, Subhash found himself fascinated with a marching soldier with a smart turn out and gun. Sometimes, he found himself as a soldier in his fancy world. However, his imaginary soldier was no cruel, atrocious or inimical soldier of the British; rather he was a duty-bound and compassionate social servant. He came to know that there is provision for military training for students. It pleased him like never before, he grew eager to join it. He was somehow prepared to see the discriminatory conduct, like it was in any missionary school, but his doubts were soon resolved. He found that the military training, given in the college, was uniform for all the students; no discrimination was practised in their drill, arms training and appointments. He started to achieve military training from the year 1918.

In this connection, Subhash had said, "Sitting in the company of sages and hermits following the spiritual path is quite different from obeying the commands of a military officer. This training proved a boon for me because it enhanced my energy and self-confidence. Those days, rifles were stored in Fort William in Calcutta. Only English officers and soldiers were allowed to enter there; ordinary Indians were not allowed to go there. However, the students undergoing military training were allowed to enter it to draw rifles. On the first day, when we marched to Fort William to draw rifles, it appeared to me that we could take the better of those officers and workers who were habitual of treating Indians as slaves. This was an important turning point in my life. This brought a number of changes in me, which had a positive outcome later."

How right Subhash was! It was on the basis of this training that Subhash Chandra Bose became strong from the inside; later this became the foundation to unnerve the British empire.

First in Examination

Subhash now focussed on his studies. He had created a niche for himself among his professors on the basis of his hard work, perseverance and competence. Now, he was recognized as a hardworking student as against a student who had once been expelled from a college. Looking at his focus, his professors often said, "We have seen a great number of students, but Subhash stands apart. He is little worried of the outcome, his only mission seems to deliver cent per cent. We are confident that his selfless action would result into the most excellent outcome."

The examinations were drawing near, all students were busy with their studies. Subhash too studied late into the night. He knew that his father wanted to see him pass with good scores, and he had decided to achieve this feat.

In 1919, Subhash appeared for his graduation, and coming true to everybody's expectations, he passed the examinations in the first division. He attained the second position in the entire Calcutta University. His family was effulgent at his accomplishment.

Now, he was a popular student. His professors took pride in him; they admired him all the time. Even newspapers carried articles on his success.

Subhash had proven his competence and made his father take pride in him.

□

12
Father's Challenge

Subhash was more and more inclined towards his studies now; he decided to go for further education. He had analyzed the events of the past few years and poor condition of India; and this made him turn away from Philosophy. In post-graduation, he chose practical psychology as his subject. Explaining this, he said, "Philosophy is the best tool to know higher human faculties. I have studied them deeply, but later I realized that it was rather more necessary to know the lower faculties too, since it is meaningless to think of the high without having known the low. Psychology unfolds all layers of human behaviour and disposition, so I selected this subject."

However, luck had something else in store for him. The future was unfolding its mysterious knot slowly.

Jankinath was busy carving the career of his promising son. He talked to Sharat Chandra in Calcutta about a plan. This plan impressed Sharat Chandra too. He approved of this saying, "Your idea is good, Subhash cannot have a better opportunity than this. It would brighten up his life, but it would be better to ask him first."

"All right, we'll talk to him about this today," Jankinath said exultantly.

Sharat Chandra, like an obedient son, only shook his head in affirmative.

In Calcutta, Subhash stayed with Sharat Chandra. When he returned from college in the evening, Jankinath made him sit near him and said tapping his head, "Son, you have attained the first division to make us all full of joy. We have never been happier than this before."

"This was all your blessing and affection; I could achieve this feat only due to your care," said Subhash softly.

Jankinath said, "Subhash, I have done my duty and nothing else. You have accomplished this only due to your hard work and focus. You are a master of infinite competence, and you have proved this; but, son…"

"But…but what, father?"

"Subhash, listen to me carefully. I want you to touch the zenith such that the world bows before you. Those who thought you in the wrong should be ashamed of their thinking. Those who think you mischievous and useless, should see a new Subhash before them whose light will make even the sun trivial; I want to see you touch the skies. I wish…" Jankinath paused for a while and resumed his talk, "I wish you appear in the Indian Civil Service (ICS), and clear it too."

Subhash's mind was electrified.

"Indian Civil Service!" he could utter only these words.

Little caring what was going inside Subhash, Jankinath continued, "Clearing the ICS examination is the proudest thing for a youth. There are only a few people in India who could pass this. I am sure that you can pass it with your untiring dedication."

"But its examination is held in London. How will you make arrangements for my going there and staying there?"

"You don't have to worry on that count. I, together with Sharat Chandra, have arranged for everything. Your ticket for the ship sailing for London next week will be acquired. You have to just prepare for your departure."

"But, father, I want to do my M.A. in psychology; it is difficult to leave all this and head for London just now," he protested mildly.

Jankinath gazed at him and then said earnestly, "You want to lose upon a golden chance for M.A., do you? People want to have this opportunity, and you are talking to skip it! Your M.A. degree will not stand you in good stead, so give it up, and decide upon going to London. If you pass the ICS, the postgraduates will be running about you."

Subhash hung his head down. At this, Jankinath said, "Subhash, keep in mind that in no other job you find more money and honour; this will make you keep yourself and your family completely satisfied."

Subhash, who was influenced by the ideals of Vivekananda, had never been attracted to greed, attachment, honour or pleasures, nor had he dreamt for luxurious life ever. When in youth, other people were busy gathering fortunes through all tricks, Subhash had aimed at serving the country and society. This was the reason that this offer of riches and happy life from his father only made his soul to protest.

'Is man's life meant for selfish pleasures? Is there no duty beyond the family fold? Can a man continue to live a life of joy and luxury even when people around him are reeling under penury and starvation; is it justified to earn riches by exploiting the poor? No, I cannot be a part of this inhuman system. I want a life which is rooted in ideals, which is replete with truth, justice and humanity.'

Subhash's face was firm with his inner sentiments. He said, "Father, I will not appear for the ICS examination."

"What...!" Jankinath was stunned at this reply. "You are not impressed even after all this discussion. Can I know what is the reason behind this?"

"The British are inflicting atrocities on the Indians; they are sucking the blood of poor farmers and workers in the name of taxes; our people are being discriminated against in every way; we are treated inhumanly at public places, offices and parks; our starvation and epidemics have deprived the country of its prosperity; and the British government is alone responsible for all this malaise. Its policies have only degraded the system. In my view, there can be no greater sinful government system; so my soul does not approve of becoming a part of the very system."

Jankinath knew the inner feelings behind these words. He felt that the young man was under the influence of nationalism, like revolutionaries and social reformers. He did not want

Subhash to jump into the freedom struggle and spoil his life. Therefore, he explained to him, "All these appear very fascinating in books; they have little value in practical life. Shake off the fancies and accept the hard reality of life."

Jankinath could not waver Subhash from his resolve in an affectionate manner. When he failed, he blew his final stroke, "Well, Subhash, why don't you clearly say that you have no confidence in your ability. You are afraid of appearing in the examination because you know that it is beyond your capacity. You are timid, but want to hide this timidity in the garb of nationalism and humanity. I am a fool to have high hopes from you. Had I realized this, I wouldn't have spent so much of money on you."

The stroke was severe, Subhash's heart was pained at this. He said, "I am no timid, nor am I scared of failing in the examination, but I..."

Jankinath cut him short, "There is no use talking like this. If you are no timid, then prove that you can pass it."

The challenge went against Subhash's wish, yet he could not have borne with the burden of its negation, so he accepted the challenge and said, "Father, I'll go to London, please make arrangements for that."

The very next week, Subhash Chandra Bose sailed for London; his relatives came to see him off, but Subhash knew that this voyage was to prove himself, it might not have any relation with his future.

□

13

Accomplishing the Goal

The ship set out from Calcutta on 15 September 1919 and arrived in London on 25 October. The voyage covering over one month was a period of meditation and contemplation. He utilized this period to study deeply the life and doctrines of Indian philosophers and social reformers. In this voyage, he set before himself some goals. As soon as he set foot in London, his mental conflict transformed into a firm determination.

By the time he arrived there, the new academic session had already begun. He ran from pillar to post in order to secure admission in Cambridge in the first week of November. As only eight months were left for the examination, he set down to study earnestly. Here, he befriended Dalip Kumar Roy, C.C. Desai, N.K. Siddhant, Kshitij Prasad and other talented students, who all went on to achieve distinctions in their respective fields. This peer group soon created a unique identity for itself.

Eight months seemed to have passed in no time. The examinations began in July 1920. Subhash appeared in them all with total dedication. Now, he waited for the result. And finally, this day too knocked at the door.

The result was declared on 20 September, 1920. The name of Subhash Chandra Bose stood fourth in the merit list; he had attained the first position in English composition, he had excelled over the English students in their own mother tongue. The entire atmosphere resonated with his success. He received congratulatory messages from different places in London and India. Everybody admired him.

When Jankinath came to know of his son's achievement, his joy knew no bounds. He decorated the house with lamps and flowers, he donated money to the poor and distributed sweets.

'The son has achieved the goal that his father set for him,' this thinking made Prabhavati's eyes moist. She was rendered sentimental thinking about the golden career that lay ahead for Subhash.

However, in the distant sky, the divine light had set out towards the earth to amalgamate its flame in a Yogi.

Discontented Mind

Subhash was still reeling under the tempest of thoughts, his heart was yet unquenched. Delineating the emotions of his discontented heart, he wrote a letter to Sharat Chandra. He said: "I don't know whether I have gained or lost by clearing the ICS, but it satisfies me that this pleases my parents and family members. It is a moment of achievement for having attained the fourth place, yet this also remains true that I am not mentally happy. If I have to join this service, it would be the source of the same helplessness under which I had to head for London. This service will no doubt give me honour and good salary; it will give me comforts and luxuries of life; it will give me a status of a high government officer; I don't doubt all this, yet when I think within my heart, I tend to ask myself if this remains the aim of my life. And then I go on to infer that this type of life, devoid of any suffering and struggles, is without any purpose. When my countrymen are striving for hand-to-mouth existence, will this service not make me a link in the chain of slavery to bind my own people? I want to serve my country, and it would not be possible for me to do while remaining in this service. In such a situation, I seek your guidance."

Sharat Chandra knew his younger brother well, and how he thought. He now guessed that Subhash would have to be prevented from giving up this post, so he tried to make him understand and wrote: "Subhash, I respect your sentiments and ideals, but mind you that in this service, you will be able to serve the country in a better manner. You will be able to make use of the government machinery for the country's welfare; therefore, you ought to think deeply before taking any decision."

The suggestion was appreciable, but Subhash felt himself burdened. His heart was restless to get emancipated, so he expressed this restlessness in his letter on 26 January, 1921: "You say that I should serve the country while serving in the government machinery, but then, this will not make me work freely and without prejudice. And then, the greatest question pertains to my principles. I cannot overlook them in order to become a part of the unjust, atrocious, oppressive and cruel system. The only question standing tall before me is: Should I give up all my ideals and principles in order to accept the government post, or should give up everything else in order to devote myself to the service of country and society. At this moment, I feel that the path of renunciation and service is the most adequate. I know this decision of mine will trouble you and your dreams will be shattered; but I have to think above all this. I have to think beyond the narrow scope of the family. I am fully confident of your principles, so I write what resides in my mind. I know you will try to convince Father in this matter."

He wrote another letter on 16 February, 1921, in which he mentioned his future course of action: "There is no task too difficult to do for a youth like me; there are a number of fields in which thousands of youths are needed such as teaching, journalism, village development, social service and the like. The National College will easily hire me for a teaching job, while the *Swaraj* paper will create opportunities for me to work with it; both these jobs are to my liking; so I am little worried about my future. My only desire at this moment is to dedicate myself in the service of the nation living a simple life and to strengthen the Indian freedom struggle. After due thought, I have decided to resign from my post, because I feel myself a slave working under the British government. I have acquainted Father with all this. Now, I await his approval."

Father's Warning

The father grew restless when he came to know what his son wanted. He knew about Subhash's views on social reform and patriotism even when he had sent him to London, but he thought that his connection with patriotism would be severed abroad. He never hoped this type of behaviour on his part; but the situation had not improved; he was rather still mad after nationalism.

Jankinath responded in harsh terms: "What type of foolish decision this is! Only the most fortunate get the prestigious ICS job, and here you are the one who is bent upon kicking away your fortune. If you lose this opportunity, you will find nothing but aimless wandering all your life. Therefore, I advise you to focus on your future and leave the useless talk. In it lies your good. However, if you still want to hold on to your decision, I will no more compel you to change it; however, if you do so, you must not expect for any financial assistance from me, because I cannot waste any money on an adamant and stupid son."

He had thought that it is simply unimaginable to live abroad without money. He thought that this warning letter could force him to change his decision; but a father had misunderstood his own son. He had overlooked that Subhash was a massive boulder which had not learnt to shatter even under adverse situations. This warning from Father made him still more resolute.

On 6 April, 1921, he wrote to his brother Sharat Chandra again: "Suffering and renunciation—these two are the pillars of *Swaraj*, and a free and strong nation is built on them. If we are ready to dedicate ourselves for this cause, nothing can prevent to transform the abstract concept of freedom into a concrete reality. Today the country requires a youth from every family, the one who could dedicate himself for the motherland. It is unfortunate for the country that no ICS officer has shown this courage before; so I fail to understand how I can deprive me of this. I understand that this will amount to insurmountable hard work, poverty and starvation, but I am ready to bear with all that. I can resign on my return to India, but for this, I will have to sign the format which symbolizes slavery for me; and in that case, it will retain me here until December or January, in place of present July. This period of six months is unbearable.

It will not matter much whether I resign now or one year later, but the Indian freedom struggle will certainly be adversely affected by this delay. Renunciation for the country is a matter of pride for any Indian, but Father wants to hold me back from this out of his love and affection. He has warned me of financial constraints, yet I cannot change my decision now. I have vowed that I will sacrifice everything for the country, and I will remain firm on this decision."

Resignation from Post

The day of 22 April, 1921 was marked in the history of India for the unparalleled sacrifice by Subhash Chandra Bose. It was a historical day on which he resigned from his ICS post. This brought about a tempest; Subhash had given up a prestigious post with all smiles on his lips, it was a post which made people strive for. This action on his part was no short of amazement for the English even.

When the news of his resignation was published in newspapers, sharp criticisms and remarks were expressed. His professors, friends and even some English well-wishers tried to reason with him.

Those days, Sir William Duke, Jankinath's friend and former Commissioner of Orissa, was the Under Secretary of state for India. As he knew about Subhash's competence, he was confident that he would become a useful officer for the British government in the future; so he too tried to convince him, he said: "If you think that you have achieved the purpose for which you arrived there, and resign, then it is simple stupidity. This decision will shatter all your family's dreams."

"The goal has been achieved, no doubt, but this was not my destination; my final goal is to attain freedom for my country and re-establish Indian glory. I don't accept to become an oppressor on this government post; I am firm on my decision."

"All right, if you don't want to be a government servant, don't do it, but just wait until you have returned to India. Consult your father with a calm mind and then decide what you should do." Sir William made his last bid.

However, this did not succeed. Subhash could not waver from the decision he had taken. This proud man did not like to form part of the oppressive government; he had transformed himself into a nationalist who refused to be under the command of the government. It was clear that Subhash did not want to compromise with his ideals and nationalism; for him, the country was above everything else, and he was ready to give up his comforts and facilities.

The voyage from passing the examination to resigning was now complete, so it was no more useful to stay in London. Therefore, he packed up for his return journey. The ship arrived in India on 16 July, 1921, and Subhash smeared motherland's soil on his forehead and thought himself lucky to do so.

□

14
Rise of Gandhiji

On the horizon of Indian politics had risen a star in the form of Gandhiji. He had created a place for himself in South Africa and now he was in India to join the Indian freedom struggle. Soon, he was known as the highest national leader. The moderate leaders followed in his footsteps of non-violence and *Satyagraha*. The Congress, which was until then seen as a weak party, emerged as a strong political party.

Until now, Gandhiji put before the government his demands in a peaceful manner. He believed that the demands would be considered sooner or later. This thinking led him to support the government during the First World War too. However, the Rowlatt Act, *Jallianwala Bagh* massacre and prejudiced findings of Hunter Committee made him rethink his strategy.

Non-cooperation Movement

Right since beginning, Gandhiji was opposed to violence and extremism; but he did not want that his moderate and cooperative conduct should be construed as his weakness. Therefore, he wanted to put his case before the government firmly, and it was to be in the form of *Satyagraha* and non-violence. Therefore, in the Congress Session at Calcutta in September 1920, he proposed to start the Non-cooperation Movement. The goals determined under this included the following:

- Return of all titles and honours awarded by the British government.
- Boycott of legislative councils and elections.
- Boycott of government functions.
- Refusal to recruit in the army.
- Boycott of law courts.
- Boycott of educational institutions.
- Boycott of foreign clothes.
- Picketing at liquor shops.

To propagate the movement in every nook and corner of the country, he toured different places and held mass meetings in order to awaken people.

In no time, the movement became massive. Students boycotted schools and colleges, advocates boycotted law courts, government servants too joined the fray. Bonfires of foreign goods and clothes were raised; women picketed before wine shops to compel their closure; the workers, washermen and maids refused to work in the households of the English people.

Influence of Gandhiji

When Subhash returned to India, the movement was at its peak; the entire country was echoing with the name of Gandhiji. His power of struggle and ideals had impressed the Indian masses greatly. His amazing achievement in South Africa against the English had raised the hopes of Indian people that he would do something magical in India too. Subhash too was influenced by this charm. He explored his principles sitting all alone.

Discussing the personality of Gandhiji, once Subhash said: "By 1920, the legal system had become inactive so far as social welfare of India was concerned. Armed revolution was at its peak. It seemed almost impossible to seek agreement by peaceful policies. The country needed an able and powerful leader, who could command the national movement in a novel manner. Under such complex situations, a great leader came to the fore who possessed resolute determination, and he was none else but Mahatma Gandhiji. He knew that the coming times will assign him the responsibility of leading the new age, so he dedicated himself in deep meditation in order to accumulate energy within himself. His politeness was not a deception, nor did he lack any power to struggle; he possessed firmness in his voice and he had gathered all people under his flag."

"If all Indians were united, freedom can be attained within one year," this statement from Gandhiji filled Subhash with excitement. He was eager to meet him. Those days, Gandhiji was staying in Mani Bhavan in Bombay (now Mumbai) and was running the movement from there. Therefore, Subhash set off to Bombay to meet him.

Meeting with Gandhiji

Subhash stopped at the main gate of the two-storey building.

Reading the nameplate as Mani Bhavan, he felt a sense of satisfaction.

A Congress worker came to the gate when he found a stranger there. He asked about him.

"My name is Subhash Chandra Bose, I want to see Gandhiji."

The worker glanced at him and then asked him to wait before going in. He returned after a while and said in a soft tone, "Follow me, I'll lead you to him."

They crossed the corridor and entered a large hall. On the carpet spread on the floor was sitting a great man, the man who made even the British government frightened; he was the man who made the English struggle before him in South Africa; the man whose one call started an era of nationalism and sacrifice in the country; the man whose glowing face with a pair of round spectacles and bald head, weak body adorned with only a *dhoti*, was sitting before him. Finding Gandhiji before him in a concrete form charmed Subhash.

Gandhiji was surrounded by his followers and was discussing with them. When he looked at the door and found him standing there, he said with his popular smile: "Come Subhash. I welcome a nationalist like you."

"Do you know me?" Subhash was amazed.

"Who will not know the Subhash, who kicked away his government job at the call of conscience, who gave up his material pleasures and chose a thorny path, who is determined to serve the country at the cost of his family? The sons like you are seldom born. Come, sit beside me."

Subhash sat near him.

"How did you come without any prior intimation?" asked Gandhiji.

"I wished to be in your company for quite some time; moreover, I have a number of unresolved queries in my mind, which compelled me to come here. The first desire has been fulfilled, now I am hopeful that my questions too will be answered."

"I shall try to answer all your questions."

Their discussion commenced from the plan which Gandhiji had chalked out to bring about the fall of the British rule; he was curious to know about it.

Gandhiji explained the plan and said, "Our goal is to cripple the government by a peaceful movement. Under this, we will lay emphasis on non-cooperation with the government. Besides, we will boycott foreign goods and clothes and will propagate *Khadi*. If the government implements any oppressive law, we will threaten it not to pay any taxes in protest. It will help the Indian cottage industry prosper while it will shut down the sources of financial gain for the government. In such a situation, the government can be compelled to fall in the favour of Indians."

Subhash listened to him with complete attention. He found many of the contentions reasonable, but he doubted others. He said about these: "I failed to understand what he wanted to do with them. Either he did not want to reveal it then, or his plan was vague in the future context. Still I satisfied myself that I was not mature enough to understand him well."

The two sons of India, Gandhi and Subhash Chandra Bose, both wanted to free India from the oppressive British; but the truth remains that both of them treaded the paths of different ideologies. According to Gandhiji, the proper path to attain freedom was through reforming the government or effecting a change of heart in it. For this, he conceived the path of fasting, demonstrations, strikes and prayer meetings. On the contrary, Subhash was of the view: "No external power could help India selflessly; if Indians did not make efforts themselves, their hope for independence would remain a mere pipe dream. The national movement is not like a sudden eruption which could sweep away the jails built over ages. It requires building through collective energy, brick by brick, on the basis of which the foreign rulers could be challenged." It was evident that the views of both the leaders were dissimilar and their working methodologies were guided in different directions. The experienced Gandhiji could well understand his feelings. He wanted that Subhash had a proper guide who could utilize his energy to direct it to the proper direction. Thinking this, he advised the young Subhash to meet Deshbandhu Chitranjan Das.

After this, their conversation came to an end; the meeting was over.

□

15
Attainment of Teacher

Chitranjan Das belonged to the well-known Das family of Bikrampur, Dacca (Dhaka, now capital of Bangladesh). He had done his law from London and was doing his law practice in Calcutta. Soon, he was a busy man and was counted amongst the famous barristers in the country. His success can be guessed from the fact that his monthly income even in those days was as much as one lakh rupees, but this condition did not prevail for long. His heart rose in rebellion against the poor condition of India and oppressive British policies. Gradually, he became popular as a patriot; the direct evidence of this was seen in the year 1909 when he saved Aurobindo Ghosh, who was accused of being part of Alipore Bombing case. With this case, he came to be known as Deshbandhu Chitranjan Das. With time, he gave up his legal practice and became active in politics. He kicked away his income running into lakhs of rupees, this speaks volumes of his renunciation, indomitable courage and determination.

In the political class of Calcutta, Chitranjan Das emerged as a powerful and able leader. As a result, he was counted amongst the strong pillars of Indian politics.

Subhash knew of Deshbandhu Chitranjan Das from his college days. He had contacted him for legal advice when he was expelled from the college. He was so impressed by his personality, thinking and patriotism that he, during his London sojourn, maintained contacts with him through letters. In his heart, he had accepted him as his Guru. This was the reason that when Gandhiji suggested his name for a promising youth like him, Subhash grew restless to meet him.

As soon as he reached Calcutta, he went to see him.

Deshbandhu knew that Subhash had given up his government job at the call the conscience, and that now he was resolved to tread on the path of revolution. He thought himself grateful on meeting him, he welcomed Subhash with open arms.

During the conversation, Subhash referred to his talks with Gandhiji and asked, "His plan is beyond my grasp, what do you think his clear goal is?"

"Gandhiji wishes to establish unity, justice and ethics in the country. His principles revolve round truth and non-violence, and he follows them. His greatest feature is that he wants to trouble the government through peaceful means. This is the reason that the entire country follows when he starts a movement, but it makes his policies vague and cannot be implemented fully. As a consequence, the British counteract even more vigorously. This is right that the Indian people are second to none when it comes to courage, tolerance, renunciation and sacrifice; it is not at all impossible to throw the British out if all Indians have resolved for this; but this is also true that we are still ignorant of the right method of struggle. The goal of the freedom can be achieved if the right method is adopted at the opportune moment."

Subhash was assimilating every word within himself, he expressed his opinion, "The people trust Gandhiji the most; no doubt he is our respectable leader. Our paths and ideologies might be diverse, yet we have to bridge this gap in place of further widening it. We have to unite in order to fight for freedom. I am confident that only this joint effort will prove useful against the British."

This talk of twenty-four-year-old Subhash impressed Chitranjan Das greatly. He expressed pleasure and said, "Few people possess the art of equal opinion for different efforts made by different people for the attainment of a sacred goal, and you are one of them. I can see the future India in you."

Subhash Chandra Bose had found a political Guru in Chitranjan Das, while Deshbandhu too was joyous to find a diligent and intelligent pupil.

Later, Subhash Chandra Bose wrote about this meeting thus: "During our discussion, I came to know that he knew well of the future plan. His goal and the plan to achieve it were fully clear to him. He was a great man who was ready not only to sacrifice everything of his own, but also ask others to sacrifice theirs. In his view, being young and having energy was a sign of positive viewpoint. I was extremely happy to meet him, because I had found my guide."

In November 1921, Subhash became a member of the Congress.

Responsibility of College

In the opinion of Deshbandhu, education was a vital tool by which the dormant people of the country could be awakened. He used to say: "When people are educated, the darkness of their ignorance and injustice would automatically disperse, because then they would realize their rights and duties and struggle for them." With this view in mind, he had founded Calcutta National College.

Most of those students had taken admission in it were those who had boycotted government schools and colleges at the exhortation of Gandhiji and were connected with the movement in one or the other manner. Their minds were replete with political agitation and national consciousness. Chitranjan Das wanted to use them in national interest. Therefore, he had formulated the system of 'National College' to implement his views.

The college had excellent educationists. They didn't teach students to flatter the government, rather they aimed at cultivating the spirit of nationalism and patriotism in them in order to construct national leadership. The curriculum here did not follow the monotonous English-oriented course which sang eulogies for the government, rather it was an interesting, lively, knowledgeable and developed curriculum, which contained India's history together with world history. Not only this, it acquainted students with the struggles that had been undertaken right since the arrival of the British to India's slavery.

Thus, Calcutta National College became the largest source of nationalism for the youth.

Chitranjan Das wished that the college should be assigned to an individual who could execute work at both academic and political levels. His sight fell upon one person, who was none other than Subhash Chandra Bose. Subhash did not need to prove his eligibility; he had passed the ICS; moreover, he was full to the brim with a sense of duty, and as a member of the Congress, he had shown his efficient working methodology. Therefore, after due thought, Chitranjan Das appointed him the Principal of National College. It was no trivial achievement for Subhash, immediately he set down to work according to the expectations of the college.

Volunteer Chairman

Towards the close of November, a meeting of Bengal Provincial Congress Committee was held, in which the executive officer and Chairman of the Rashtriya Swayamsevak Sena Dal were to be appointed. All members of Calcutta Congress were present including Subhash, who had taken a seat at the flank.

Chitranjan Das, the Chairman of the committee, was in the chair. He addressed the members: "I propose the name of Subhash Chandra Bose for the post of executive officer, he is the hardworking and dedicated Principal of National College as well as a member of the Congress. I hope, no one of you will have any objection to this."

Subhash was rendered speechless at this proposal, while the meeting was enveloped in a pin-drop silence.

A volunteer opposed, "Subhash has been a member only for a few days, it would be unreasonable to assign him such a vital responsibility. A number of senior members are present here who have worked for the committee devotedly. You can assign this responsibility to anyone of them."

Chitranjan Das smiled and said, "We need, not a senior member, but a young and hardworking volunteer for this post who can infuse vitality in the youth to join the national movement. I am confident that Subhash will come true to our expectation. Thinking this I have selected him. As far as senior members are concerned, it is their duty to guide the youth."

The argument was logical, so the protestor sat down silently, and after that, no one else objected to this. The proposal was approved by the members.

Before Chitranjan Das read out the second proposal, he glanced at the committee members and then said clearing his throat, "As is known, we need a Chairman for the Swayamsevak Sena Dal, he should be a young man physically and mentally. Therefore, I propose the name of Subhash Chandra Bose for this post too. He has obtained military training, which will help to keep the youth workers in shape and strength."

The members clapped to approve this second proposal too.

The very next day, The *Statesman*, a prominent newspaper of Calcutta, published the details of this meeting. Commenting with reference to Subhash Chandra Bose, it wrote: "The promising officer that the government had lost, has been found by the Congress. His competence could have been a mark of achievement for the government, but now the same energy has been unleashed to reign in the government."

□

16
Visit of the Prince

The First World War had been over three years ago, but it had unleashed upon the worlds unruliness and disorder. Even England was not untouched by this; as a consequence, its position in India was shaken. Taking advantage of this situation, the Indian leaders intensified the Non-cooperation Movement. The entire country witnessed protests, demonstrations, strikes and mass meetings against the government. People resigned from government posts, students boycotted schools and colleges, even the domestic helps gave up the household duties with the English and became part of the movement. It had its adverse impact on the government machinery. The situation became so hopeless that the decline of English rule was predicted in near future.

The government worked with insight, and decided on the programme for Indian visit of the Prince of Wales (Edward VIII). The idea behind this was to display English glory and power in order to strengthen its position in India. The English wanted that the moderates could be drawn in the government's favour by giving a few basic facilities; it would weaken the opposition and the government's image would improve.

Keeping this in view, a plan was made to implement the constitutional reforms of Montague-Chelmsford Committee during the royal visit. The programme was chalked out, and it was propagated in the entire country in order to create curiosity among people. The government was confident that it would make the Indian people think about something else than the movement. However, they did not realize that the public protest had taken a vicious turn because of the government's apathy and oppression; people were agitated, their blood was boiling. They wanted justice, they wanted their motherland free, they wanted the sinners to pay for their actions; they wanted to glorify the Indian pride and honour; therefore, they too got ready to welcome the prince in a fine manner.

17 November, 1921. The Prince of Wales set foot on the Indian soil with British glory and magnificence. This was the first occasion when a member of the British royal family had ever come to India; but everybody was well aware that all this was a mere formality.

Peace prevailed all around. The British were happy to see everything going as per the plan, but as the royal entourage proceeded towards the town, thousands of people could be seen standing on either side of the road. They had black flags in their hands and they were shouting 'Go Back'; this was their way of welcoming the royal dignitary. The entire country was bound in a bond of unity.

The entire country witnessed a strike that day. All shops, markets, schools, colleges and offices were closed down. The government was taken aback by this unprecedented demonstration; it never hoped for such a massive protest; but now it was under pressure. In a bid to control the situation, the police and demonstrators grappled, leading to only merciless killing of a number of demonstrators.

When the royal entourage left for Delhi, it witnessed a Bombay-like situation. As soon as the Prince arrived in Delhi, the entire town resonated with the slogans of, 'Prince Go Back'. Nothing but black flags and aggressive crowds could be seen everywhere. Some bid was made to bring the situation under control, but the situation was really volatile. One could see nothing but large groups of people holding black flags. The route leading to the destination was all packed with the protestors.

Prince of Calcutta

The next stop for the Prince was Calcutta, the headquarter

of the revolutionaries. The nationalists here were agitated following the incidents that had taken place in Bombay and Delhi. They wanted to reply to the government in kind. Calcutta Congress Committee decided that it too would rise in protest as had been done in other places. Chitranjan Das assigned this responsibility to Subhash.

A few days before the arrival of the Prince, Subhash went round the streets of Calcutta with Congress volunteers and infused vitality among the people. He thundered, "We have to show to the oppressors that it is impossible to crush the honour of India so long her sons are alive. We have to stand erect like a rock to tell that we are ready to face any calamity. We are ready to sacrifice everything for the country."

The background for the boycott was complete, the masses were ready, even those who kept away from the movement had energy.

The day the royal retinue reached Calcutta, a strike was declared in the whole city. Both sides of the roads were full of black flags. All ten directions resonated with Vande Mataram. All paths were blocked, the crowd was swelling; the retinue could reach the venue somehow.

Describing the entire incident, The *Statesman* wrote: "Under the leadership of Subhash Chandra Bose, the entire town turned into a cave of patriots; you could find no one but protestors everywhere; all government offices, shops and institutions were shut. It appeared that Subhash Chandra Bose, and not the British, ran the government there. This was the welcome given by the Prince of Calcutta to the Prince of Wales."

First Imprisonment

The protest in Calcutta had surpassed as compared to other places in the country. Due to this, the entire administration had been rendered inactive; this was a pitiable situation for the government. Therefore, it now adopted oppressive policies and took harsh steps. It removed the striking workers, shops were got forcefully opened, demonstrators were arrested and sent to jail. Chitranjan Das and other important leaders were arrested, but Subhash was not a man to retract his steps. He now took over the reigns of the movement. The more people the police arrested, the more of them joined the movement. The situation became so terrible that the jails lacked room to house the prisoners.

The Congress Swayamsevak Dal volunteers staged a march on 10 December, 1921, under the leadership of Subhash. The government had already its eye on them, so it declared the march illegal and took Subhash under arrest.

The case was tried for seven weeks, and on 7 February, 1922, he was sentenced to six-month-long imprisonment. When the magistrate fell silent after the pronouncement of the sentence, Subhash said in amazement, "Only six months of imprisonment! Just this is the fruit of my patriotism! At least you ought to have seen my status before awarding me this sentence."

Whoever heard these words became an ardent devotee of Subhash. Standing erect in the trial box, Subhash was being blessed by everybody. It was Subhash's first journey to jail. He accepted it as an honour for himself, he swelled up his chest. Finally, his name too had been included in the list of the sons of motherland. The same sentiments prevailed in his family too. This is evidenced by a letter written by Jankinath to Sharat Chandra: "We all, the entire family is proud of Subhash. I was unnecessarily worried about him. It appeared to me that he would take time to mature, but he has cleared my illusion. He is capable of taking care of not only himself but also the entire country. He is the noble son whom every mother will wish to bear."

Chauri Chaura Incident

The movement had now shaken the government. All people, Hindus and Muslims and those of other faiths, were linked with this. Their unity was like a thorn in the British's eyes. However, the situation took an ugly turn which rendered the movement a failure.

On 4 January, 1922, a protest march was organised by some volunteers in a small village called Chauri Chaura in the district of Gorakhpur (now in Uttar Pradesh). The march was completely non-violent and peaceful. As the procession passed by the local police post, some English policemen deployed there commented on them. In the beginning, the protestors overlooked them, but when the insulting words surpassed their tolerance, they argued with them.

How could the brute British tolerate this retort? As soon as the inspector ordered, the protestors were fired upon, which killed a protestor right there.

Now, the level of tolerance had been crossed. The protestors were agitated and attacked the police. The policemen were only a few in number, so they hid themselves in the police post, but their last time had already arrived. It became impossible to keep the protestors quiet, they put the post to fire, which burnt to death a number of policemen.

This incident hurt Gandhiji gravely. He considered non-violence as the spirit of the Non-cooperation Movement; he was confident that he would make the British bow before him on the basis of truth; he felt that if the soul itself was destroyed, it would lead to the destruction of the entire source of energy. He felt that the country was not yet mature enough for a non-violent movement, so he declared the cessation of the Non-cooperation Movement.

Gandhiji held himself responsible for the incident that occurred at Chauri Chaura. He was taken prisoner on 10 March, 1922, and was sentenced for six years in jail on the charge of treason.

With the sudden suspension of the movement, the entire country fell in despair. Several prominent leaders, who followed Gandhiji, rose in protest. Commenting on this incident, Nehruji had said: "The suspension of the movement has made the country a victim of moral degradation. The suppressed violence was looking for an outlet which would entail in a terrible form in the years to come."

Title of Dictator

Lodged in Alipore Central Jail, Subhash too was stunned at the suspension of the movement. In his view, when the countrymen had determined to root out the British, it was an unreasonable decision to suspend the movement at a crucial turn. Though he respected Gandhiji's non-violence, yet he did not like the country being punished for its sake. He protested sharply when he said: "At this time, the command of the 'dictator' has been heeded, but this step will divide the Congress and country into two parts. When the vigour of the patriots had reached its zenith, its suspension could be termed only as a national disaster. There can be no doubt that the British will take advantage of this and emerge even stronger. The goal, which was about to be achieved shortly, now could only be achieved after a long wait."

It was obvious that the inner-self of Subhash Chandra Bose had been greatly hurt. It only tormented his trust, he was now completely detached from Gandhiji, but he continued to possess infinite respect for him.

□

17
The Radical

Chitranjan Das, Maulana Abul Kalam Azad and Subhash Chandra Bose – all three luminaries sat together in jail and talked nothing but the country's freedom. They sat for hours regularly to formulate plans for the future. They thought deeply about the future struggle and the actions to be performed under it. During these conversations, once Subhash scorned: "The moderates sitting in the legislative councils were no better than loyal protégés; their only task is to strengthen the British government's ideas. They are helping the cause of the government rather than the national movement, by which the English government has succeeded to convince them that the oppressive policies adopted by it are fully supported by the elected representatives."

With this, he suggested: "The Congress should try to grab as many seats as possible in all legislative councils, judiciary and district boards, and follow a policy of opposition from within. The elected members should be given the goal of constructive work; this will help check the evil policies of the government."

The suggestion was appreciable. Chitranjan Das tapped his back and said, "O great radical, how effective the measure you have said! When patriots join government institutions, the government policies can be brought in the favour of Indians. It will not affect the Congress's methodology and goals. This is like repaying the British in their own coin. I am confident this would initiate a new era."

He decided to implement the suggestion.

After Subhash was released from jail, he devoted himself to academic and welfare schemes, but the mind of Chitranjan Das was still busy with his suggestion.

Birth of Swaraj

In the month of December, the annual session of the Congress was held at Gaya. Chitranjan Das was appointed its President. In his presidential address, he presented Subhash's suggestion.

The leaders like Motilal Nehru, Vitthalbhai Patel and N.C. Kelkar approved of it, but the other leaders opposed it forcefully. They thought that those willing to have freedom should continue with their struggle outside the government.

As a result of this deadlock, the Congress was divided into two groups; one was those of radicals who wanted transformation, this group was led by Motilal Nehru. The other opposing group was the conventional group led by Gandhiji. Therefore, Chitranjan Das failed to manage support in the favour of the proposal. Shattered by this, he resigned from his post; rather he went a step further and resigned from the membership of the Congress itself.

Deshbandhu had accepted defeat, but Subhash was not a man to accept defeat. He motivated the disappointed Chitranjan Das with these words: "If one path is shut, we should look for an alternative path. The Congress might not have supported you, but I am confident, millions of Indians will support you. Rise and march, and you will find that you are not alone."

With this motivation, Chitranjan Das was infused with a new vitality. The same day, he met Motilal Nehru and formulated a plan for a new party. On 1 January, 1923, the launching of a new party called All India Swaraj Party was announced at Gaya. This was joined by those volunteers who were not satisfied with Gandhiji's policies. Chitranjan Das became its president and Motilal Nehru became its general secretary. Subhash took over the propaganda for the party. The goal of the Swaraj Party was to demand the imperial autonomy for India. For this, it approved of the working system of the

Congress, but it recognized the radical principle. As soon as Chitranjan Das became the President, he announced his participation in the assembly elections.

The elections were held as scheduled. Proving the truth of the prediction, the Swaraj Party gained a heavy majority. It proved its predominance in the central council as well as provincial legislative assemblies.

Giving credit for this to Subhash, Chitranjan Das said: "The party could not have tasted success but for the work that Subhash did. He went among people and brought them in his favour."

Congress Support

Gandhiji was released owing to ill-health. He was still a role model for Subhash, so on his request, Motilal Nehru and Chitranjan Das went to see Gandhiji. Mentioning this meeting, Subhash had said: "He had never directly supported radicalism, it was insignificant for the Swarajists to get elected and work for the country; but he did not adopt a negative attitude; maybe because the position of the Swarajists had grown so strong that it was no more possible to root them out. He bowed before compulsion, or he might have thought that a change in the working methodology was the need of the hour. He had silently assented his approval for radicalism, we were encouraged by this."

This statement was based on deep analysis, which could not be put down. Announcing this in the Congress Session, Maulana Abul Kalam Azad had said: "We have arrived at the conclusion that it is meaningless to boycott entry in legislative assemblies. It is in the country's interests to secure as many seats as possible. The Congress members, who have no objection owing to religious or social reservations, can contest the forthcoming elections. The Congress holds back all its propaganda against radicalism."

With this, the Congress approved the radicals.

A Young Old Man

The Swaraj Party was encouraged by its unprecedented success in the assembly elections, so it fielded candidates for

Calcutta municipal elections in 1924. This time, Subhash was nominated from Bhavanipur. As was hoped for, the party once again secured majority. Together with other prominent leaders, Subhash too had been elected unopposed, people had bestowed on him endless honour and cooperation; it was now clear that his popularity was touching new heights.

The members appointed Chitranjan Das as the Mayor, Suhravardi as Deputy Mayor and Subhash as the Chief Executive Officer. Social service and reform fell under the scope of Subhash's duties. He was now carrying out his duties earnestly.

Until then, the municipality was under the command of the British. Their chief task was to keep an eye on the citizens and collect taxes from them, but they paid little attention to urban development or cleanliness and hygiene; however, Subhash effected a change in the administrative structure of the municipality and brought about a change in its working methodology. This department until then had been a tool of serving selfish interests, but now it started to work in people's welfare. Subhash started a cleanliness system for the entire town, set up hospitals for health services, and also formulated rules for public conveniences. He also rendered invaluable contribution in academic field too. He set up the education department, which facilitated the establishment of new schools in the town. He also took steps to stop unnecessary expenditure and prohibited public facilitation functions for government officials.

The people came to feel for the first time that even government institutions could work for social welfare. As a result, they started cooperating in every possible way. These reforms transformed a corrupt and work-shirking municipality into a socially-useful institution.

Impressed by this, Chitranjan Das had said: "The credit for all this goes to Subhash alone. He possesses the vigour and perseverance of the youths as well as experience and working efficiency of the elders. In my view, he is a young old man, replete with all the positive qualities."

□

18

Saha Case

India was now ambitious to secure freedom for itself. People had been fighting against the British government using peaceful methods. In the beginning, protest was expressed through dialogue, strike, procession or fasting; but when the government was not affected, rather the extent of oppression enhanced and humanity found itself crushed under atrocities and exploitation. A section of dissatisfied youths rose on the horizon. These people were armed with guns, bullets and bombs, and came to be called revolutionaries. As contrary to Gandhiji's principles, they laid down a new rule, that was to strike back even more vehemently. "If somebody slaps you, simply cut his hand in response." These people respected non-violence, but they could indulge themselves in violent activities, if need be. They had not learnt to bear with injustice or oppression like the moderates. They could kill or get killed for the sake of the country. They held guns in hands, coffins on the heads, Vande Mataram on tongues and the heart permeated with patriotism. They were ever ready to make supreme sacrifice. This was their only identity; and freedom of the motherland was their sole goal. They became very popular due to these tasks and sacrifices.

The government was more scared of these revolutionaries than moderates, because they knew how to use force. There were occurrences when the oppressor was sniped at from a distance. Even the most hardened British officers were scared. Calcutta was considered as the headquarter of revolutionaries. The local populace looked at both moderates and revolutionaries with respect. They also rendered all possible aid to revolutionaries, whether it was related to finance or shelter.

In 1901, a police officer named Charles Taggart was posted in Calcutta. He was the first chief officer of the Indian police. It was on the basis of his report that the special branch had been set up. He reorganized the police force and made it more efficient. Impressed by his achievement, he was promoted to the rank of police superintendent in 1908, deputy commissioner in 1913 and deputy inspector general of the spy department in 1918. After this, he spread a wide network of spies to gather all related information about revolutionaries.

Unsuccessful Attempt

Taggart had been commended by the government for keeping the town free from crimes, but amongst revolutionaries, he was known as a cruel and oppressor officer. They knew him as a staunch competitor of nationalists and the one who inflicted inhuman sufferings on the nationalist prisoners in jail. On 9 September, 1915, he busted a revolutionary group in Odisha led by Jatindranath Mukherjee; it was from this time that the revolutionaries wanted to take revenge on him.

Finally, it was decided to shoot him dead. This charge was assigned to a Bengali youth called Gopinath Saha; however, he had not seen Taggart before. Taggart, an Irishman, had red hair, so this feature of his was told to Saha.

On 12 January, 1924, Gopinath sat outside the police headquarter waiting upon the arrival of the target. After some time, he found a person with red hair; he advanced ahead and shot him dead.

This occurred all of a sudden, which took the people by surprise. Gopinath was arrested. While everybody else stood rooted to the ground in fright and astonishment, Gopinath stood among them with a peaceful smiling face. However, he had committed a blunder, the dead victim was not Taggart, it was some other Irish trader, who had come to visit the headquarter in connection with some personal work; he had been killed by mistake for his red hair.

Respect to Martyr

Gopinath was tried; when in the court, he was asked to present his case, he thundered, "I don't seek any mercy, I wish that the court should award me death penalty, because it would further intensify the protest among my countrymen. Every drop of my blood will sow infinite number of revolutionaries in every house."

These words stormed the court. His courage invigorated even the timid who resolved to sacrifice themselves for the country.

The court sentenced Gopinath to death, and this brave son of Mother India kissed the knot with all smiles.

Gandhiji, the lover of non-violence, was against to this type of revolutionary activities. He did not issue any statement in this case, but Subhash thought differently. He attached importance to non-violence, but he was also impressed by fearlessness and devotion of the revolutionaries. When Saha's clothes were sent out of the jail after his final rites, these clothes were first touched by Subhash. The last words of the patriot youth had shaken him deeply. Impressed by his martyrdom, Subhash, at Sirajganj, passed a resolution in his honour.

Subhash's Arrest

The government was perturbed at the expanding influence of the Swaraj Party. It thought that the main cause of this was Subhash Chandra Bose, who had popularized the party due to his reformative policies. This had greatly checked the volitional activities of the government in Calcutta, which was rendered like a puppet in the hands of the Swaraj Party. Meanwhile, the government found an excuse to plan a conspiracy against him when he honoured a revolutionary.

On 30 April, 1924, a twenty-five-page charge-sheet was made against Subhash Chandra Bose, which compiled five letters and spy reports from ten police informers. The charge-sheet clearly mentioned: "Subhash Chandra Bose has formed a revolutionary party in Bengal, and has asked its members to make bombs and arms, so that he could take advantage of the disorder arising from the Non-cooperation Movement.

According to information, Subhash Chandra Bose is curious to start communism, he has also formed alliance with England's enemies outside India, who are ready to aid him in case of an armed rebellion. It is dangerous to set him free in national interest."

After the charges were specified, the party members were arrested under the Regulation Act.

On 25 October, Subhash was arrested in the morning hours. His residence was thoroughly searched for any arms, but nothing was found other than documents and files. The government lacked any concrete evidence, yet this fact was overlooked and he was lodged in Alipore Jail.

This injustice on the part of government agitated Chitranjan Das. He thundered, "Subhash Chandra Bose is no greater revolutionary than me, why then have I not been arrested? If loving the country is a crime, I am equally guilty. If the chief executive officer of the municipality is guilty, its Mayor is also guilty. I am aware that this ordinance has been passed with a motive to suspend a legal institution, and this has targeted the very core of the institution, that is Subhash."

□

19

Mandale Experience

Protest was continuously rising in Calcutta, the situation was becoming exploitive. In the annual session of the Congress, Gandhiji announced for implementation of the Swaraj Party's programmes. In this way, both parties stood up in support of Subhash Chandra Bose. The government knew well that this revolt could spread to the whole country if it was not tackled intelligently. Therefore, Subhash was stealthily sent to Mandale Jail in Burma (now Myanmar).

Mandale Jail had been the witness to the harsh penance of great leaders like Lala Lajpat Rai, Sardar Ajit Singh and Lokmanya Tilak. Subhash's joy knew no limits when he reached this holy land of revolutionaries.

On 2 May, 1925, he wrote a letter to Dalip Kumar Roy and expressed his sentiments thus: "Staying here has brought about a change in my views. The jail environment produces in me philosophical ideas. Whatever I have learnt here and whatever philosophy I have read here are much useful for life. If man is healthy and he gets time for contemplation, even suffering seems pleasant. Lokmanya wrote the *Geeta Rahasya* from the cell here. It is clear that despite all the shackles on his body, his soul enjoyed supreme bliss, contentment and peace. We are now following in the footmarks of a great patriot, and I feel pride and satisfaction at this thinking. I am confident that this jail will accord me spiritual tranquillity."

The system in the jail was dissatisfactory, the situation of food and cleanliness was very poor. In this context, Subhash had written: "There is all around an unhygienic atmosphere full of dirt and garbage; it is so dirty that dust particles enter your body with every breath. Food is covered in dust. During storms, the entire cell is flooded with dust. Everybody is suffering from asthma and joint pain. Half-cooked food finds passage into the body with insects and germs. The cells in which prisoners have been kept are like wooden cages, in which they feel like cattle. Often local police officers, ministers and other magistrates visit to look at us in this zoo; still I am blissful because I know that this suffering will prove to be tool for cutting the shackles of Mother India."

Right since adolescence, Subhash had been inclined towards meditation and contemplation. After he became active in Indian politics, he could not undertake these owing to lack of time, but now in jail he had abundant time at his disposal, so he was drawn to these once again. He deeply studied Burma's history, culture, historical and political background and geographical location. Staying with political prisoners of Burma, he also came to know about guerrilla warfare in detail. Besides, he also took out time to think over future plans.

Gradually, a new Subhash was taking shape within the four walls of the prison.

Separation from Guru

From early morning on 17 June, 1925, Subhash felt himself restless and disinterested. Some unknown fear had made his heart pitiful, he was remembering his country time and again. To concentrate his mind, he sat in a corner with closed eyes, but he found it impossible to focus his mind; just about then, a policeman handed him over a newspaper.

Subhash started reading it now.

The first two pages pertained to political and social occurrences in Burma. He turned pages with a cursory glance on them, and then on the third page, what he saw made him perspire profusely, his face was stunned, he read through the entire piece of news without batting an eyelid, and then his heart was filled with pity, his eyes streamed down with tears; his hands trembled and let go the newspaper.

The newspaper carried the news of the death of his political Guru and friend, Deshbandhu Chitranjan Das.

Chitranjan Das found himself alone after the arrest of Subhash. He felt suffocation, which resulted into a terrible ailment, and he had been badly suffering from this dreaded disease. On medical advice, he left for Darjeeling, but he could not recover from the ailment; and ultimately on 16 June, 1925, this great man closed his eyes forever.

This shock shattered Subhash mentally and psychologically. Expressing his grief, he wrote to Dalip Kumar Roy: "I feel as if I have been rendered orphan and helpless; my memory is experiencing him so closely that I find it impossible to write. I could not trust my eyes when I read the news of Deshbandhu's death, but alas, this remains the truth. It is an unfortunate moment for the country that it has lost a true son in him. No one else can ever replenish the vacuum created by him. This loss is even more terrible for the youths in Bengal." Subhash respected Basanti Devi, wife of Chitranjan Das like his mother. He wrote her too: "The entire country is engulfed in severe torture, yet the Bengali youths seem to have been deprived of leadership. At the time of this suffering, when the entire country is enveloped in dark, you are like a flame of light. Mother, bless us that we could march ahead in order to cut away the shackles of Ma Bharati."

Release from Jail

Due to polluted environment and unhygienic food, Subhash experienced a degrading health; moreover, he had been negatively impacted by the death of Deshbandhu. He suffered from throat and chest pain; he experienced difficulty in breathing, his digestive system was so bad that he found even boiled rice as hard as rock. He became bed-ridden. The jail officials were perturbed at his worsening condition.

With urgent government's approval, a team of doctors was summoned to Rangoon; this team comprised Sunil Chandra Bose, elder brother of Subhash too. After medical examination, the team submitted its report saying that he had been suffering from acute pneumonia which is changing into asthma. If he is kept in this moist cell any more, it might be impossible to save him.

The government was not in the favour of releasing him; it was afraid that after his release, Subhash would become still more dangerous who could surpass their control, but then it was no less risky to keep him confined. He was now popular all over the country as a great man; the news of his ill-health had spread all over the country. If he died in the jail, a tempest might arise which could flow away the entire British empire. This was no little worry for the government. The government found a compromise. It said if Subhash left for Switzerland for treatment on his own expense, the government could release him.

Subhash turned down this offer. After this, he wrote in a letter to Sharat Chandra: "I don't want voluntary exile from my motherland. I have some principles, and I am struggling on their basis. Values are looked at in different ways in the market, but success or failure in life cannot be measured from physical or material viewpoint. The body can be destroyed, but no one can shatter the eternal belief. Only Almighty can tell who will emerge the victorious in the end, and He alone can tell who will witness the outcome of our efforts and toils. As far as I am concerned, I am contented with my life, and for the rest, I leave everything to fate. There is little hope for my release from jail. No one should feel bad about this. Of course, my parents will be grieved for sure, because they love their dear son. It appears to me that I am repenting for the country's sins; if I am able to rectify them, it would be a matter of pleasure for me. Ideas can never be destroyed, ideas will never dim in the memory of the nation. I am aware that this proud path will lead me to my Samadhi."

The government was undecided. Subhash's refusal had aggravated its problems. His medical examination was conducted again, but the report remained unchanged; rather his health had gone from bad to worse.

Finally, the British government had to bow down, and on 16 May, 1927, Subhash Chandra Bose was released from jail.

□

20
Re-constitution of Swaraj

Subhash was in jail for two years, six months and twenty-one days, after this he returned to India; however, the political circumstances had undergone a complete change. A number of large and small parties, in addition to Congress and Swaraj parties, had been formed under the leadership of well-known leaders. The extremists had a great influence. Revolutionaries like Chandrashekhar Azad, Bhagat Singh, Rajguru, Sukhdev, Jatindranath, Shiv Varma, and Kundanlal were popular all over the country. All of these worked according to their respective ideologies and policies, yet they all aimed at the common target, that was to secure freedom of the motherland. Their efforts had awakened the masses, the rebellion was sounded even in remote areas. The Indian freedom struggle was being discussed at the international level, which pressured the British government like never before.

Subhash was satisfied at seeing the flame erupting into a massive fire, but two incidents made him restless. The first was the formation of the Muslim League. Some Muslim members of the Congress had given up the membership and formed this new party; it was being headed by Mohammad Ali Jinnah. In Subhash's view, the formation of this party was not right, because he considered encouragement to fundamentalism as venomous; and the foundation of the Muslim League was the outcome of this venom. The British government had played the policy of divide and rule, and this had created havoc in the country. When the Muslim members left the Congress, there was a rift between the Hindu and Muslim communities. Those who talked about brotherhood, love and mutual cooperation a few days ago, were now thirsty for each other's blood. Its aftermath could be seen in the form of communal riots, which destroyed the unity of Indian society.

The other incident which perplexed Subhash was the poor condition of the Swaraj Party. Chitranjan Das had died and Subhash was in jail. In such a situation, the party was now led by Motilal Nehru, but under the prevailing situation, he found the management of the party very hard. He was struggling alone at all three levels: government policies, conspiracies by loyal ministers and betrayal of party members. Motilal Nehru looked at both Hindu and Muslim communities equally, his policies were meant for well-being of both communities, but it worsened his position. The Hindus blamed him for Muslims' appeasement while the Muslims considered him a Hinduist. In this way, he had lost trust of both communities. The main cause of disastrous defeat of the Swaraj Party in 1926 was just this.

Subhash decided to improve upon the condition. He was elected as the President of Bengal Provincial Congress Committee, and set down to reconstitute the party.

Simon Commission

To control increasing anger in India and to satisfy Indian leaders, the British government, in 1919, formed a committee under the Chairmanship of Lord Montague and Lord Chelmsford. This committee recommended some reforms, but they were illusionary in nature; it only tormented the country, and now the revolutionaries became influential. On 8 November, 1927, the British government announced to send a seven-member commission to India to study the situation. The commission was assigned to visit different places in the country in order to ascertain the difficulties being faced by people, and accordingly it was to submit its recommendations. The commission was headed by Sir John Simon, a well-known barrister of London, so this came to be called Simon Commission.

It was shocking to note that no Indian member had been included in the commission. It was clear that the government wanted to mislead the Indian masses once again. The newspapers severely criticized this policy.

The Hindu Mahasabha, Muslim League and other liberal organisations had already formed their minds to boycott the commission. The Congress too announced its decision to boycott it in Madras Session held in December 1927. The session appointed Subhash Chandra Bose, Jawaharlal Nehru and Shoib Qureshi as the general secretaries and assigned them the responsibility to hold protests and demonstrations on a larger scale.

Declaration of Revolt

Simon Commission arrived in Bombay on 3 February, 1928. As per the plan, a countrywide strike was announced and the commission was welcomed with black flags and slogans 'Simon go back', everywhere it went. This unprecedented demonstration shocked the government. The commission finished its work in a tense situation and left for Delhi, but the situation was the same. Nothing but a sea of people carrying black flags could be seen everywhere. The entire route from the station to the destination was filled with black flags.

The commission was welcomed in Madras in a like manner, but now the English could not tolerate it any more. They shot at the crowd and killed three demonstrators there.

In Calcutta, Subhash led the protest. He announced a public strike and also held a bonfire of foreign goods. He visited every province with Pt. Nehru and invited people to protest. His speeches filled the youths with vitality, who now supported him with open arms. As a result of his efforts, the protest in Calcutta was successful.

Martyrdom of Punjab Kesari

The fifth stop for the commission was at Lahore. Angered at police atrocities in Madras and Calcutta, the extremists wanted to respond in kind, but they finally decided that they would protest against it the way it had been earlier planned. The boycott protest in Lahore was the responsibility of the Naujawan Bharat Sabha.

The day the commission was scheduled to reach Lahore, Lala Lajpat Rai was leading the protestors at the railway station. He was accompanied by tigers like Bhagat Singh, Sukhdev and Dhanvantari. The police did not want to give them any relaxation, so atrocities were unleashed once again. On the orders of Scott, a police officer, the policemen started the cane charge.

But this time, the struggle was vociferous, in which Lala Lajpat Rai was gravely injured. This hurt Lalaji not only physically but also psychologically; he suffered from mental agony more than physical hurt. Finally, on 17 November, 1928, Punjab Kesari Lala Lajpat Rai succumbed to his injuries and left for heavenly abode.

When Subhash came to know of this sordid incidence, he was shocked. Paying him tribute, he said: "Today Mother India has lost one more of its brave sons. After Deshbandhu, this is the second most grievous hurt, which has hurt our souls too."

Support to Youths

In Maharashtra Provincial Congress Session, held on 3 May, 1928, Subhash Chandra Bose supported the youth saying: "The youth power will have to be united and cultivated with political awakening; they will not only work but also dream; they will not only destroy but also construct; where we fail, they will succeed. They will construct a new India for you which will be based on the failures, re-efforts and past experiences. Today's youths are not ready to sit silently by assigning leadership to the senior leaders, they are no more ready to follow the leaders like dumb animals. They have to build a free, great and powerful India. They have taken upon themselves this task and they are ready to face its consequences too. We will have to carry forward our thinking in order to find solutions to the basic national problems. We will have to struggle without hope for any cooperation from others. We will have to listen to criticism and censure for the sake of our selfless tasks. We will have to present ourselves to bear with unwarranted, unnecessary enmity from our own."

In fact, Subhash accepted the youths as the nutrient for clean and powerful politics. According to him, it was a grave mistake to keep the youths aloof from politics, which could impede the country's freedom. Like Chitranjan Das, he too accepted the significance of the youths in politics. In this context, he had said: "Take any problem in a slave country, and when you sit down to analyse it, you will find a political problem in its foundation. Life lies in entirety. Education and politics cannot be separated. Human life cannot be segregated into categories. Even independent countries don't ban their students from taking part in politics, because it is from them that political thinkers and able diplomats emerge." If Indian students don't take active part in politics, where will we get our leaders from? How will we train them? "Participation in politics is essential for building their character and vitality. The universities should wish to build men of good character in place of bookworms, gold medalists and office clerks; only they can make the country great."

Workers' Beloved

Until the initial months of the year 1929, the world was facing deflation. Its evil effect could be seen at the international level. With the fall in prices, the Indian exports fell to the minimum level. The large factories in Bombay had been shut down, due to which workers faced unemployment and starvation. Struggling with this terrible situation, the workers sought the refuge of communists, and inclined towards struggle under their leadership. Looking at them, workers and labourers in other towns too joined the struggle. As a consequence, protests and strikes were held all over the country.

To repress the worker movements, the government enforced the public safety ordinance, and workers started to be arrested. Subhash too was a supporter of workers' welfare and rights. He appealed to them: "Workers should maintain mutual cooperation, so that the movement is strengthened. If we succeed in uniting workers, farmers, the oppressed, youths, students and women, a mass energy can be produced in the country, which can be ultimately used in making the freedom movement of the Congress successful."

In the capacity of the defence committee, Subhash also met the workers held in Meerut conspiracy case. He grew very popular among workers, and he was soon identified as a workers' leader.

□

21
Government's Stratagem

After the failure of Simon Commission, the government had no other alternative but to hand over the charge of formulating the Constitution to India. However, it knew well that the main parties of India – Congress and Muslim League – mutually differed, and a controversy could be created between them in order to bring the situation back under control. Thinking this, the government asked the Indian leaders to prepare a draft which was acceptable to both Hindus and Muslims.

The Congress called an all-party meeting at Delhi in January 1928, in which over one hundred representatives took part. Unfortunately, it ended without a conclusion. The greatest obstacle in it pertained to the rights of the minorities.

The same year in March, the meeting was held again. This time, two sub-committees were formed, but they could not arrive at any decision due to Hindu-Muslim differences.

This conference was held on 19 May, 1928 for the third time, in which a committee was constituted with universal consent, and it was assigned the responsibility of preparing a draft for the Constitution. Motilal Nehru was appointed the Chairman of the commission. It had nine other members including Syed Ali Imam and Shoib Qureshi.

Nehru Report

The committee submitted its report three months later, which came to be known as Nehru Report. Its main recommendations were as follows:

- India should be given the status of an autonomous state.
- The form of the central government should be federal, in which the governor general should appoint the prime minister and six ministers. The remaining powers should vest in the centre.
- There should not be any separate electorate for any particular community. The minority voters will not be given any additional importance. They have been granted concession under the Government of India Act of 1915. The minority communities have been given reservation where their strength exceeds a minimum of ten per cent.
- Muslim reservation is not feasible in those regions where their number falls short of ten per cent.
- The central council will have one-fourth Muslim representatives.
- If the committee approves that Sindh is economically self-dependent, then it can be separated from Bombay.
- The North-West Frontier Province should be given the provincial status.
- Hindi should be the main official language. The language of the federation is Indian which could be written in Hindi, Urdu, Gujarati, Marathi, Telugu, Kannada and Tamil scripts. Permission to use English will be accorded.

Demand for Complete Swaraj

Gandhiji wanted that the prevailing imperial self-rule could be accepted until a definite time when Britain could concur with Nehru Report. If England did not concur with this report until the close of 1929, or cancelled it, the Congress will have all the rights to start the non-violent movement.

However, Subhash was not satisfied. He knew how wicked the British government was, so he presented a constitutional amendment demanding complete Swaraj. Speaking in this favour, he said: "I am afraid that I am moving an amendment to a proposal presented by Gandhiji, but it is necessary because the young generation of India has vowed to get the country freed. We respect our senior leaders. At the same time, we wish that they should identify the changing times and march with it."

"The present youth knows its responsibility, and also realizes that it is the future heir. It has to get the country freed. The youth is ready to confront any difficult situation with this new awareness."

"In your original proposal, you have given a time of one year to the British government. Are you fully confident that the Imperial Swaraj could be achieved within this period? Pandit Motilal Nehru has himself expressed reservations on this count in his speech. We know the reality, then why should we kneel? Why should we keep our national flag at half mast for one year? Why should we not declare fearlessly that we have no more faith in the British rule, and we are about to take some harsh measure?"

"Right from the commencement of the national movement, we have imagined of freedom in the form of complete Swaraj, and not in the form of a colonial state. Being a colony has never been our goal, nor could it be acceptable to the countrymen. We should remind ourselves that the youths are the inheritors of the future."

"India is prosperous in human and physical resources. It has also stepped out of its infancy, which has been time and

again imposed on it by the foreign rule. The Indians are mature, they are a superior race. There is no essential uniformity between India and Britain, by which we could think that India could accept a colonial status linked with the British empire; rather we can guess more harm if we keep connected to it. If India remains under the British imperial rule for long, it would never emerge out of its inferiority complex. So long it is a part of the British empire, it would be extremely impossible for it to oppose any British selfish policies. The only proper diagnosis for India's weaknesses is Swaraj, and to be able to do this, we have to work for freedom."

"In conclusion, I request that the only alternative with us lies in accepting this amendment of complete Swaraj so that we may preserve our self-respect. Its approval will not disrespect any of our leaders. Respecting leaders is one thing and compromising with principles totally another. I entreat you earnestly that this amendment proposal may be approved in order to infuse the youths with a new consciousness."

This amendment proposal divided the Congress into two groups. The group under Gandhiji wanted the report approved in its original form, while the other group, led by Subhash and Jawaharlal Nehru, supported necessary reform in Nehru Report. Both sides agreed to come to a decision by a majority vote.

Most of the members were in the favour of the amendment; however, the situation underwent a change at the time of voting. They voted in favour of the original report lest their support should annoy Gandhiji, who could quit politics.

Consequently, the proposal fell. This was no new thing for Subhash. He knew about Gandhiji's influence on the members. So he was not wavered and accepted this defeat, but at the same time, he predicted: "We have no other alternative but complete Swaraj. Tomorrow, if not today, the Congress will have to accept this alternative of complete freedom."

Delhi Declaration

In England, the Labour Party came to power in 1929. The Congress was confident that it would work for the welfare of India, so it raised the demand for colonial autonomy more forcefully. When pressured, Viceroy Lord Irwin consulted the then Prime Minister and Sir John Simon, Chairman of the Commission. After this on 31 October, 1929, the Congress demand was accepted and declaration was issued to this effect, which said that the British government was firm on its decision to grant colonial autonomy towards constitutional progress of India. A round table conference would be held soon, which would decide upon the future course of action.

This declaration made the Congress leaders happy. They called a meeting in Delhi and signed the approval declaration. This declaration came to be called Delhi Declaration; however, three members protested and stayed away from this, they were Subhash Chandra Bose, Dr. Kitchlew and Abdul Bari.

Opposing the declaration, Subhash had said: "Gandhiji is trapped in a diplomatic stratagem. The Viceroy's memorandum, when gone through deeply, does not manifest anything which could encourage us. It is like betraying the people. The government could deceive the countrymen. It would harm the people greatly. Therefore, I request all people to oppose this."

However, this opposition remained ineffective, the party was not moved by this.

Lahore Session

In December 1929, the Congress Session was held at Lahore. It was expected that Gandhiji would chair it, but he proposed the name of Jawaharlal Nehru. This decision shocked everybody. The Congress had senior leaders like Vallabhbhai Patel and Rajendra Prasad; it was improper to appoint Nehru by superseding these leaders. Fifteen out of eighteen Congress provincial committees opposed this, but Gandhiji remained unwavering on his decision. Finally, the committees were compelled to support the young Jawahar as the President.

The session proposed for a complete Swaraj resolution by Nehru, which was seconded by Gandhiji; it stunned all members again. They were now supporting the same demand which had been disapproved while demanding colonial autonomy. The reason was clear that no progress had been made in the intervening period. They now knew that the government was doing only paper work to trick them. All those doubts that Subhash had expressed during Calcutta Session as well as Delhi declaration now stood before the Congress in a concrete form.

On 31 December, 1929, Jawaharlal Nehru hoisted the Tricolour and announced complete Swaraj. With this, the resolution was passed with universal concurrence. Gandhiji himself wrote the pledge for complete Swaraj, which had to be taken at ten o'clock in the morning on Basant Panchami, that was on 26 January, 1930.

The Congress had no concrete plan to attain the goal. In such a situation, Subhash proposed that the Congress should form a parallel government and unite youths, students, farmers and Harijans under it. It could make the movement impressive.

As had transpired before, this resolution too fell.

□

22
Democratic Party

Subhash Chandra Bose considered the Congress's policy of appeasement as an obstacle in the path of realization of the goal. He opined that it not only harmed the national pride, but also revealed organisational infirmity of the Congress, which only goes to benefit the British government. Therefore, he expressed his opposition from time-to-time in order to bring it on the right path, but this revolting nature had displeased a number of members. They were the ones who believed in conventional principles and wanted to follow the beaten path, and looked down upon any innovation. When the leftists supported Subhash, they completely went against him and decided to keep him apart.

Finally, the opponents played their trick at Lahore Session. The list of the members in the Working Committee excluded the names of Subhash and other leftist leaders. Looking at his popularity and hard work, the All-India Congress Committee wanted his name included in the list, but the Gandhist leaders did not allow any change to the list.

Subhash did not accept defeat. His mantra for life was to struggle right until the last breath, only then it could transform into the greatest pleasure of life some day. He went on abiding by this principle. He accepted that struggle might be prolonged, its form might be degrading, yet one should stick to his goal, because selfless action is more important than a selfish motive. It is enough if you are heard by people; it should not make much difference whatever the stage.

Neglected by the Congress had certainly perplexed him, but he was not disheartened. His goal was clear, the need of the hour was to look for a new path, and he found it himself.

On 2 January, 1930, he founded the Democratic Party. Explaining its purpose, he said: "We support both moderate as well as extremist political movements. We have no place in our heart for flattering the British or seeking their mercy. Our only goal is freedom of the country, and we are for struggle rather than appeasement."

He sought the blessings of Basanti Devi, wife of Chitranjan Das. He wrote to her thus: "Like the past occurrence at Gaya and compelled by the rigidity of majority, we have constituted a new party. I pray God that the soul of Deshbandhu may lead us and your blessings may inspire us."

In response, Basanti Devi wrote: "God has fixed the zenith of greatness for you, wherefrom the remaining world would seem a manikin. It has opened new vistas for you. Advance doubtlessly, my blessings are always with you."

Birthday Gift

Having constituted the party, Subhash set down to propagate it. On 9 January, he addressed a labour union and said: "We all have to work for freedom. Mutual cooperation will bring us nearer our goal. Therefore, I urge upon all workers, labourers, farmers and low-class craftsmen to come forward and strengthen the movement, so that their economic exploitation by the government could be checked."

The Congress decided to celebrate Independence Day on 26 January, 1930 all over the country. In Calcutta, this responsibility was borne by Subhash. As a duty-bound member, he prepared for it. Those days, his daily routine was very busy. He had to tour different provinces, meet numerous people, address public meetings, lead marches, and the like, and he was doing justice to all these responsibilities.

His activities warned the government. In the past, the government in Calcutta had suffered much when the situation was brought under control somehow. It did not want the same situation to recur, so it issued arrest warrants on the basis of an old case.

Subhash had his birthday on 23 January, 1930. On this occasion, he was leading a demonstration when he was arrested. When people opposed, the police cane charged, injuring a number of people. Subhash too suffered from injuries. He was blown so mercilessly that he was rendered unconscious for an hour. It was in the state of his unconsciousness that he was carried to jail. The very next day, he was presented before the court where he was sentenced to one-year rigorous imprisonment.

The patriot Subhash Chandra Bose had been given an adequate birthday gift by the oppressive government.

Disobedience

As planned, Independence Day was celebrated on 26 January. On this occasion, Gandhiji issued a declaration which stressed opposing the government for violation of human rights. People concurred with this vigorously. Meanwhile, the Salt Law was implemented. On 2 March, 1930, Gandhiji wrote to Viceroy Lord Irwin asking to drop this law, but his request was overlooked.

In protest, Gandhiji conducted the *Dandi March* and violated the Salt Law. With this, the Disobedience Movement started. Bonfires of foreign clothes were raised, government schools and colleges were boycotted; the entire country resonated with Swadeshi.

It was like an open challenge for the government. It issued an ordinance and declared the martial law.

Thousands of *Satyagrahis* were lodged in jails. The police fired at a number of places killing several people. Gandhiji was leading the movement, he was taken under arrest on 5 May and was brought to Yarvada Jail. Jawaharlal Nehru, the Congress President, and Motilal Nehru, the officiating President, were lodged in Allahabad Jail.

Post of Mayor

In jail, Subhash's health deteriorated, so he was released

by the government unconditionally on 25 December, 1930. As the lion stepped out of the cage, he was once again ready to struggle. People were happy to find their favourite leader amongst them. It appeared to them as if a warrior had returned to defend them.

Those days, the election for Mayor was being held in Calcutta. Subhash filed his nomination and won the election by a huge margin. His popularity was so remarkable that even the defeated candidates felt it a moment of glory for themselves. One of them went to the extent of declaring that the people of Calcutta had able leadership now and it would not be long before their fate changes.

After he took the oath of office as the Mayor, Subhash said: "We have no hatred or enmity against the English race, nor is our struggle based on any selfish interests. Our struggle is aimed at our rights and freedom. This is a struggle for the country's pride, it is a struggle for the Indians' self-respect."

Subhash considered every section of the society as important. He opined that neglect of any one section is enough to render the national movement unsuccessful. Whether they were craftsmen or labourers, whether they are students or women – he worked for the coordination of all these sections. With this goal in view, he founded the Bengal Swadeshi League so that coordination could be established among traders, industrialists, social institutions as well as the lowest sections of the society.

This was how the resolute Subhash was marching ahead for attainment of freedom for the country.

□

23
Round Table Conference

Looking at the intensity of protest, the government held the first round table conference in London on 12 November, 1930. It was being chaired by the then British Prime Minister, McDonald. A total of 89 members attended it, including 16 members each from Indian princes and British party, and fifty-seven from British India. The conference was convened to discuss the problems as well as demands of the Indians, but the strange thing was that no member from the Congress, the largest party then, was invited.

On the first day, different matters were discussed and a number of sub-committees were formed, but it revealed differences among Indians. All of them stuck to their respective demands. In the lack of unity, the English got an opportunity to exploit the situation. As a result, it resulted into nothing for the Indians.

Subhash was looking at this conference minutely. Remarking at the outcome, he scorned: "The round table conference has given the Indians two bitter pills in the name of security and federal structure. To conceal bitterness, they have coloured the pills in sugary coating. The British Prime Minister has very cleverly said that if India accepts its protection and federal structure, it would be given a responsible right in the centre. It provided our respectable liberals more than they wished and they are satisfied with this. They did not even once ask what would be our actual responsibility after we accepted the conditions of protection and federal structure. The fact remains that our liberal politicians have returned from across the ocean with only assurances."

Gandhi-Irwin Pact

The government was oppressing the campaigners, but it was not possible to retain national leaders in jail for long. This action on the part of the government was being criticized not only in India but also abroad. Therefore, Viceroy Lord Irwin proved intelligent when he initiated action for the pact, and a meeting was convened in Yarvada Jail. It was participated by Gandhiji, Sarojini Naidu, Jawaharlal Nehru, Motilal Nehru and two members from the Congress Working Committee. Lord Irwin invited Gandhiji to Delhi for a dialogue, which he accepted.

After a long discussion over many days, finally on 4 March, 1931, Gandhiji and Irwin signed a pact, known as Gandhi-Irwin Pact. The following important decisions were included in it:

- Gandhiji will hold back the Disobedience Movement.
- The Congress members will take part in the second round table conference in London.
- Foreign goods will be boycotted in a peaceful manner.
- The British government will retract its emergency ordinance.
- The people living on sea coasts will have liberty to make salt.
- All those prisoners will be released who are in jail due to their participation in the movement or some nominal violence in this connection; but they should have not committed any other kind of violence or incitement for violence.

In the evening on the following day, Gandhiji held a press conference and explained: "Personally I feel that those guilty of violence should not be in jail too, but I am confident that people will realize that I could not have asked for their release; however, it does not mean that I or the Working Committee members are not at all bothered about them."

The Congress was not averse to the pact, but Subhash was. He reacted sharply: "Even those following Gandhiji blindly are stunned at the pact. They had never imagined that Gandhiji would agree on such conditions, but the pact has been signed. Gandhiji too is not unaware of reality. He has accepted in the press conference that none of the parties should think that it has won in it. In my view, this was not the adequate time for the pact. It should be taken as a bane rather than a boon, because it would obstruct the path of freedom. Had the struggle continued for a few days more, its result could have fallen in our favour."

Sacrifice of Patriots

People had been awaiting Gandhi-Irwin Pact for long curiously, mainly because of Bhagat Singh, Sukhdev and Rajguru. This trio was popular for their revolutionary activities. They had revenged the death of the popular leader Lala Lajpat Rai and had won the hearts and confidence of people. Now their only goal was to sacrifice themselves for the freedom of the motherland. Their resolve to march on this path had shaken the government. These three were now in jail following their daredevilry of throwing a bomb in the assembly and murdering Saunders. The court had already sentenced them to death.

Subhash Chandra Bose did not want to loose these enthusiasts. He knew that the responsibility for struggle for freedom lay on their young shoulders. He hoped that the pact would include a provision for their release; unfortunately, there was no trace of any such thing in it.

In their meeting, Gandhiji had talked to Irwin on this matter, but Irwin had expressed his inability to take any concrete step. He said that this case was under Punjab provincial government and he could not do anything in it. At the same time, he assured that since several people had appealed for mercy, he would consider the matter seriously and get their sentence changed into life imprisonment.

However, this assurance was a mere deception. The government tricked and hanged all three of them just a day before.

This incident disappointed Subhash deeply. He said: "Gandhiji should have remained firm on this issue. It could have saved the patriots. The motherland has been deprived three of its able sons in Bhagat Singh, Sukhdev and Rajguru. The moderates tend to call them terrorists, but in the times to come, they would realize the importance of their martyrdom. They have not died, they have become immortal. They have attained the status of *Dadhichi* (a sage who sacrificed himself for a noble cause) in India's freedom struggle. They were the souls of revolution, their flame would keep burning in our hearts at all times."

□

24
Naujawan Bharat Sabha

To guide revolutionaries and to unite them in a common bond, Bhagat Singh had founded the Naujawan Bharat Sabha in 1926. It provided the revolutionary movement a broad arena which was aimed at keeping in touch with the masses using different means and to acquaint them with the objectives and ideas of the revolutionary movement. The objectives which the Sabha had specified grew very popular among people. These were as follows:

- To unite farmers and workers for establishment of a complete republic.
- To infuse in youths the spirit of patriotism on the basis of nationalism rather than on the basis of religion or caste.
- To aid them in their economic, social and industrial movements which could assist in creating anti-communal ideas as well as in the establishment of a republic which could be an ideal institution for farmers and workers.

After the martyrdom of Bhagat Singh, the Naujawan Bharat Sabha was rendered as good as leaderless. Its members were in search of an able leader who could match Bhagat Singh in ideals, principles and renunciation; who was filled to the brim with the spirit of patriotism; who could have conquered over the fear of death; who was determined to sacrifice everything for the country. Not everyone is armed the spirits of renunciation, bravery and courage to the extent as to smilingly embrace death.

Therefore, all of them set their eyes on none else but Subhash Chandra Bose.

It was only Subhash who could pass the test that Bhagat Singh had laid down by his high standards of patriotism. It was only who could make up the loss of Bhagat Singh; it was only he whose arms were strong enough to strengthen the organisation and lead the country. Therefore, the members of the Sabha approached him to become the President.

He thought over the matter for a few days and then concurred.

On 27 March, 1931, Subhash Chandra Bose took the oath of office as the President of the Naujawan Bharat Sabha. In his presidential address, he said: "We will have to free ourselves of all types of social, economic and political bonds; it means freedom of all kinds. I want a socialist republic in India. Until reformative or revolutionary elements are blossomed, we will not get freedom, and revolutionary elements cannot be awakened until we are not able to give a new message, which could transmit from heart-to-heart. The basic shortcoming in the Congress plan and policy is that our leaders' minds are abundantly vague and full of mental conflict. Their programmes are based not on some basic principles, but on adjustment; like adjustment between a master and a servant; like between a capitalist and a worker; like between a high class and a deprived class; like between a man and his wife. If we have to achieve our goals, we will have to take up some important steps; for example, to mould farmers and workers according to socialism; to unite the youths to create a disciplined volunteer force; to draw out women from homes to put them on the path of social work; to boycott foreign goods in order to adopt indigenous goods; to create new literature for setting up new ideas and new ideals; and so on. If we follow the programme with determination, there will not be any conflict with the Congress leaders. Our mutual tension can weaken the people and strengthen the government. India is the foundation stone of the world's edifice; after freedom, it would root out imperialism from the world. Get ready and jump into the struggle for freedom, so that humanity might live. This is the call of the time."

Subhash delivered a number of speeches after he became the President, all these were aimed at uniting all sections of the society, and he was tasting success in all this too.

Failure of Round Table Conference

Under Gandhi-Irwin Pact, the second round table conference was held in 1931. The delegation for London had been selected at Karachi Session itself. This delegation was being led by Gandhiji, and other members of this included Sarojini Naidu, Madan Mohan Malviya, Mohammad Iqbal, Sir Mirza Ismail, Ghanshyam Das Birla, S.K. Dutta and Sir Syed Ali.

Just two weeks before the conference, the Labour government had been uprooted and it had been replaced by the Conservative Party government. Lord Irwin had been replaced with Lord Wellington as the new Viceroy. In this way, the circumstances did not favour India, still the Indian delegation arrived in London with high hopes.

On the first day of the conference, the new Secretary of State for India, Sir Samuel Hoar clearly told Gandhiji that India could neither be given freedom nor colonial autonomy. He went to the extent of refusing to accept Gandhiji as the representative of India. All efforts proved futile, the government had changed its colour.

Tired and desperate, Gandhiji returned disappointed.

The entire country was stunned. It was only Subhash Chandra Bose who hoped such kind of behaviour in England; so instead of blaming the British government, he criticized Gandhiji. Though he respected him much, yet he did not shy away from criticizing his loose and vague policies and working methods.

Issuing a statement he said: "It was the gravest mistake to send Gandhiji alone as India's representative. He was the only one fighting for the pride of India in an assembly of one hundred people. His position was like that of an Abhimanyu who was tricked into a stratagem. He found the situation unfavoruable. Had he been accompanied by some nationalists, or had he gone to England a few weeks earlier when the Labour Party government was in power, the outcome could have fallen in India's favour. Lack of able advisors and lack of a clear plan made his entire plan vague. Gandhiji failed to impress the British imperialists and British people. His simplicity, eloquence, politeness, respect for the opposition – all these manifested his internal weakness, leave alone impress the British Prime Minister. It was in the country's interests to reveal all things, but then his prestige has been harmed in the opinion of British politicians. Gandhiji repeatedly proposed for seeking hearty cooperation from the British, and it created a pitiable condition in the conference. Had he talked in harsh terms like that of Hitler, Mussolini or Stalin, Britain could have well understood everything and they would have bowed before him."

Recourse to Oppression

Gandhiji returned to India on 28 December, 1931, and with this, he announced to start the Disobedience Movement again. For it, 1 January, 1932 was fixed.

The government was ready to tackle this. It issued an order to strike at the Congress committees. The government was more threatened by Subhash Chandra Bose, who had led the movement in 1930 and took it to its zenith through his able leadership; therefore, the police arrested him first on 2 January, 1932. After this, Gandhiji, Jawaharlal Nehru, Vallabhbhai Patel and other Congress leaders were arrested in a planned manner. With time, an ordinance was promulgated to arrest people all over India.

In two months' time, thousands of people were sent to jail. The situation turned so bad that the government had to change its policy. Now, those who took out demonstrations or protests were caned. The Congress was declared an illegal organization and its meetings and demonstrations were prohibited. The native publications were also banned.

However, the movement kept spreading in place of shrinking; people grew fearless to hold bonfires of foreign goods and hold protests through demonstrations, strikes and meetings.

Communal Award

The Disobedience Movement was at its peak. All repressive measures had miserably failed; at this, the British government formulated a conspiracy to divide the Indian society along religious and caste lines and thus weaken the movement.

According to the plan, the then Prime Minister, McDonald announced a disputed electorate system called Communal Award. This award was based on caste-based electorate, in which the Harijans could vote only for the Harijans; they had no right to vote for any candidate belonging to any other caste.

This was how the government schemed to augment its power and divide the country into small segments.

The Communal Award was implemented on 8 August, 1932. Agitated by this communal step on part of the government, Gandhiji commenced his fast unto death.

Impressed by this decision of Gandhiji, Subhash wrote in his admiration: "Irrespective of the impact of Mahatma's fasting on the countrymen, it has proved to be a boon at the international level. Until now the world knew of only one Indian problem, that was the foreign rule of British over India; but now, the top leader of the national movement had proved that there was yet another issue, and that was internal dispute, which is so important for the country that he has risked his life for this."

Subhash was able to get news of Gandhiji's fast in the jail. The falling health of Gandhiji was a matter of anxiety for him, but he himself was fighting ill-health; at this time, he could only offer prayers for Gandhiji.

□

25
Expelled Yogi

Subhash's health was turning from bad to worse with every passing day. The cell where he had been lodged was a very small, dirty and dusty cell. There was no provision for prevention from hot, cold or rain. As a result, his old ailment raised its ugly head once again. He suffered from stomachache; he also showed the symptoms of tuberculosis. However, the government was not in favour of releasing him, so he was shifted to Jabalpur Central Jail in the name of improvement. There, the doctors examined him and recommended to send him to some warm place.

The situation in north India was even worse; the movement was running in a great flow. The revolutionary parties were attacking police stations to help the prisoners escape. The Naujawan Bharat Sabha too was a revolutionary party, and its members could attack the jail to secure the release of its leader. Therefore, Subhash was transferred to Madras to keep him away; however, his health did not improve even there. After keeping him in Madras for a few days, the police brought him to Bhuvali Sanatorium in United Provinces, and then to Lucknow.

Subhash's condition was deteriorating continuously. Referring to the medical report, the jail superintendent wrote to the government: "Subhash Chandra Bose's condition is aggravating quickly, and its main cause is the lack of necessary facilities and cleanliness. According to doctors, he could be saved by a change of climate and an adequate treatment. If attention were not paid to him, we would have to be ready for any untoward news."

It was clear that the moist dark cell of the jail was like a death cell for Subhash. The death was laying its icy hands to trap him, while the government was adamant not to release him. It knew well that Subhash would jump into the movement the very moment he is set free. It could not have struck its own feet with the axe by doing this. As a precaution, it tried to put his health-related information under cover.

However, the government had forgotten that there were other millions of Indians watching him. The Indian masses were not unaware of the atrocities being inflicted on Subhash at the hands of the jail officials. The group of jackals had surrounded a lion and was awaiting his death. Whenever his ill-health was reported, people grew agitated. They did not want their favourite leader to die the death of a coward. As a consequence, a demand for his release was raised in every nook and corner of the country; the government was severely criticized through demonstrations, strikes and public meetings.

This time the circumstances were different. The country was burning in the fire of movement. When pressured, the government played its old trick. It once again put the condition that if Subhash agreed, he would be sent abroad for treatment at his own expenditure.

It would be better to go abroad than to die in this dark cell. It would be advantageous in two ways; first, the world would come to know of the Indian situation and England would be made amenable at the international level; and second, aid could be sought from the Indians living in foreign countries. Subhash Chandra Bose earnestly planned for the future and then he consented to proceed abroad.

The government had got what it wanted. In no time, Subhash was brought from Jabalpur to Bombay on a stretcher, and then he was mounted on a ship for Europe on 23 February, 1933.

This Yogi, who had struggled for freedom on the sacred land of India, was now expelled, and he was now proceeding to an unknown destination.

Remarking harshly at his expulsion, a newspaper wrote: "The person whose mind is behind the national movement has been sent to Europe by steamer. The person, who scared the British government out of its sleep, is the leader of Bengal Congress and Mayor of Calcutta, Subhash Chandra Bose. He is ill and weak, yet he seems to have so much of influence in the country that he was not allowed to meet anybody before his expulsion."

Meeting with Patriots

Subhash went *via* Italy to Austria and arrived in its beautiful town of Vienna. He was admitted in the sanatorium of Dr. Ferth and got back his health. It was at this place that he met Vitthalbhai Patel, the elder brother of Vallabhbhai Patel, who also had come there for treatment.

Vitthalbhai too was connected with the Indian national movement. He had led the protests and demonstrations against the British government. He was counted amongst great patriots. He favoured revolutionary activity rather than Gandhism. He disliked the methods of *Satyagraha* and fasting for freedom. He said that the British should be given a reply in their own language, only which it understood so well.

The short meeting of two patriots, possessing similar views, resulted into their friendship in no time. Now they passed most of their time in studying the prevalent political activities in India and estimation of the conditions prevailing in Europe.

Vitthalbhai was much influenced by the personality and ideals of Subhash Chandra Bose. It can be guessed from this fact that before he died in October 1933, he transferred all his property, moveable and immovable, to Subhash's name. He wrote in his will: "I have seen that patriot, he is infused with unshakable faith and is bent upon struggling for India's freedom without any compromise. All my property should be given to him; he is free to utilize this money for the progress of India in any way he deems fit."

However, Sardar Vallabhbhai Patel challenged the will in the court. The case ran for six years after which Subhash's claim to his property was cancelled. After his victory, Vallabhbhai handed over the property to Gandhiji for social work.

Joint Declaration

Gandhiji decided to fast for self-purification. With this, he also declared to suspend the movement for some time. Consequently, the government released him the same day. Gandhiji also appealed to release other political prisoners and lift the ordinance, but it was not sanctioned.

When Subhash came to know of this, he was perplexed. He issued a joint declaration with Vitthalbhai and sent it to India. It stated: "The latest move by Gandhiji to suspend the Civil Disobedience Movement was the concurrence of his failure. We are of the clear view that Gandhiji has failed as a political leader. Now the time has come that the Congress should be reformed and reconstituted according to new method and new principles. This requires a new leader; because it would be injustice to him to formulate a new plan keeping with Gandhiji's long-term principles. If the Congress is able to effect this complete change, it would be the best thing, else a new party would have to be carved out of the Congress, which should be formed on reformative agenda."

The next day, the *Saturday Evening Post* wrote: "In a modern chamber of Vienna Hotel, India's two great and talented leaders – Bose and Patel – have stamped an agreement of their disaster."

Speaking about the declaration, Subhash said: "It has been issued to protest against Gandhiji's passive protest, because in our view, protest in India has fallen to such depths where active policy is needed. The failure in the round table conference has proved that history could not be changed through dialogues. The only alternative is armed rebellion, a revolt in a tense situation. The sons of India are ready to offer blood – their own as well as enemies'."

The above statement by Subhash contained a glimpse of the future which he was to create himself.

Meeting with Mussolini

In December 1933, the Congress of Oriental Studies was

set up in Italy. On this occasion, a programme was held in which a number of thinkers were invited to deliver speeches. Subhash Chandra Bose was one of them. Those days, Italy's government was led by Mussolini, who was the Head of the National Fascist Party. Because Subhash favoured socialism, so the Italian government had especially invited him.

The programme began with an address by Mussolini. After this, all guests presented their views. Subhash's speech was so

impressive that together with the present students, Mussolini himself was also charmed. He saw a powerful leader in Subhash; a leader who could defeat Britain and rule over India.

At the end of the programme, Mussolini met him. After a formal meeting, he asked him directly: "Are you fully confident that India will be free soon?"

Subhash shook his head in affirmative and said, "Yes, of course, this is the only thing that will happen."

"Do you favour reform or consider revolution useful?" Mussolini asked next.

"In my view, revolution is necessary to get a country freed. Thinking of freedom without revolution is like seeking alms. The concept of reformative ideology will bloom in a free country, its impact remains insignificant due to slavery."

Listening to his replies, Mussolini smiled and tapped his shoulder to say: "If India's leadership lies in able hands like yours, the possibility of its freedom is quite strong."

How adequate that statement was! Mussolini knew that a country could not be kept under foreign rule for long if every citizen of it, like Subhash Chandra Bose, was ready to make every kind of sacrifice.

□

26
The Indian Struggle

Besides being a great revolutionary, Subhash Chandra Bose was also known as a writer and editor. After he came into contact with Chitranjan Das, he had started the editing work for a daily called *Banglar Katha* in Calcutta. His writing ceased when he joined the national movement; however, during his sojourn away from the country in Europe, he had sufficient time at his disposal, so he found a fine companion in the pen. The subjects of his glorious writing were not religion, music, love or fancy tales; rather he made the Indian freedom struggle his topic of writing. This was the topic on which he kept writing continuously.

Days passed by and with this, and he did not realize when a large pile of papers was ready with him. These papers comprised description of the freedom struggle, his ideology, political circumstances in India, as well as review of different well-known leaders of India. This treatise was the inference of all the incidents taking place in the freedom struggle over the past several years; he had written them all objectively.

This book was published in November 1934; it was titled by Subhash Chandra Bose as *The Indian Struggle*.

Until then, the other countries did not know the actual condition of India. Even their media was aloof from the reality of the Indian freedom struggle. Whatever they knew were from the books by English writers, which covered more and revealed little. However, this book unveiled the truth by removing the dark of ignorance.

He wrote: "The Indian struggle is not a selfish rebellion started by a few communities or people, rather it is a fight for pride, respect, self-dependence and freedom. It is a struggle against imperialism. India, bound in the shackles of slavery, is trying for independence. This struggle is not confined to only a specific community, rather every citizen of India is its part. It is the collective struggle of the nation, in which people of different faiths and castes have come together. Indians little care what the world thinks about them. They have set their goal, and they are ready to make any sacrifice for its realization. The British oppression in India cannot continue for long. Soon the day will dawn when the Indian forehead will be daubed with the sign of victory, and it will be known in the world with respect and honour."

The Indian Struggle had presented the Indian side so firmly that the western countries could now know the actual circumstances prevailing here. They now knew the wickedness of England. As expected, the book became extremely popular in Europe.

Reviewing the book, the prominent newspaper of England had written: "Possibly this is the most interesting and impressive book written on Indian politics by an Indian politician. If this is compared with the books written by the generation of leaders during Lala Lajpat Rai's times, it would become amply clear that Indian political thinking has been rapidly evolving. The book becomes all the more important because the author is the youngest of the three most important personalities of Indian politics. Though the book deals with Gandhiji a little harshly, yet his followers too would accept that his review is not based on antagonism. Bose has also written on other aspects of India. The author is deeply interested in evolution of socialism, worker movement and trade union movement. In brief, it can be said that the book evokes our interest in seeing Mr. Bose taking part in Indian politics."

Ban on Book

The book was selling like hot cakes; the newspapers and journals carried articles in appreciation of the book and its writer. The book was now recognized as an excellent book on politics and was popular in countries like Poland, France, Italy, Turkey, Austria, Germany, Netherlands and other countries. Even the readers in England were not untouched by this. The book had set a high record of sale there. However, despite all this appreciation, this book could not reach India directly.

The government had already seen the impact of Subhash's pen. It had seen that his words could draw out flames from cool ambers; therefore, it declared the book as unlawful and banned it in India fearing that might flare the movement more forcefully.

However, this ban only worked to create more curiosity about the book. Its ban failed to check its entry into India. This book made to every nook and corner of India in stealth.

Father's Death

While Subhash Chandra Bose was propagating his ideas in the form of his book, back in India, his father was seriously ill. His health was taking a beating with every passing day. Subhash was so absorbed in his tasks for the nation that he did not find time to serve his parents; but they never complained about this. They knew that Subhash had been born for the country; he had dedicated himself to the service of the motherland. They had never tried to destroy the penance of their son by talking about family duties; however, when Jankinath sensed his last time, a telegraph was sent to Subhash.

As soon as Subhash got this information, he grew restless and little caring for his own health, he headed for India.

But the fate had not decided in favour of the father's meeting with his affectionate son; he waited for him and finally on 3 December, 1934 he gave up his life. Subhash came to know of his death at Karachi. He was tormented at this news, he controlled himself anyhow and reached Calcutta the following day.

People thronged the airport to welcome their favourite leader, but as soon as he stepped out of the aeroplane, he was seized by a military party. The government had instructed that he could not meet anybody other than his family members. He was banned from going anywhere. All those papers, books and magazines that he carried with him were all seized too. He was informed that any violation of this order would result into a seven-year-long rigorous imprisonment together with a heavy fine.

Subhash reached his residence in a closed police car.

The man who never wavered in the face of hardest troubles, who bore with all suffering with a broad smile on his face, who bore with the inhuman torture in the jail without a complaint, even he could not control himself when he came near his father's dead body, he burst out crying like a child. It was at this hour that a new feature of Subhash was revealed, only this hour revealed that this rock-like man had a delicate heart within, his mind was the source of emotions and love, which manifested themselves through the tears that streamed down his eyes.

Subhash was under house arrest until the final rites. The police surrounded the house with great caution. No one outside the family was allowed to come near him.

Subhash stayed in India for one month and then he set out for Europe once again.

□

27
Experience of Love

According to scholars, "Love is a delicate experience which is related to the mind. It can be felt only by the man who attaches importance to the mind as well as the heart; who respects deep emotions of the mind." The word 'love' is so simple and pure, but it is very complex to analyse it. If defined from philosophical viewpoint. Love is a blissful feeling, the experience of which blooms the innate self of man; and then he draws a sense of love and aesthetics towards the most trivial objects of the universe.

The concept of love is not a modern idea, rather it has been identified as an important organ of the nature over centuries. According to the Vedic and Poranic scriptures, the very origin of the universe is based on this feeling of love. Love originated in man from different emotions. Without love, the world might not have the ideals like affection, humanity, civilisation, social coordination, compassion, morality and the like; without it, the universe could have come to an end before it could evolve or expand. Love becomes all the more important because it has no streak of selfishness. It is that invisible energy that binds people together, so love is given the utmost importance. Whatever its form, man cannot keep himself aloof from it. This fountain streams out for one or the other being.

Something of the sort occurred with Subhash Chandra Bose too.

Emilie Schenkl

Due to preoccupation in Europe, Subhash needed a secretary who knew English well. He asked an Indian friend living in Vienna to look for a secretary for him. He introduced a young woman named Emilie Schenkl. Her proficiency and command over English impressed Subhash greatly, and he appointed her as his private secretary.

Emilie Schenkl was born in Austria, but she was intelligent, hardworking, compassionate, tolerant and emotional, just like any Indian girl. Those days, Subhash was ill, this lady served day and night. Besides, she also well managed all his burden of work. It was under her care and untiring service that Subhash could overcome his illness.

Emilie had helped Subhash greatly when he was busy writing *The Indian Struggle*. Appreciating her in this connection, he once said: "I have no hesitation to admit that it was difficult to complete the book without Emilie's assistance. Her contribution is commendable in this."

Wedlock

While Subhash was impressed by simplicity and intelligence of Emilie, she too had his great personality in the depth of her heart; they understood each other's sentiments; they respected each other's views; they possessed uniform views about life. In fact, it was only love which was drawing near two people who hailed from different countries and backgrounds. This love did not hanker after selfishness, greed, indulgence or fame; it possessed only affection, purity, trust and attachment.

A few years later, when Subhash went to Austria again for treatment, they married.

As there is no evidence available, there are some misconceptions about the year and place of marriage. According to some historians, it was performed in 1937 or 1941 in Austria, while other scholars opine that it was solemnized in 1942 at Berlin. Still others doubt if it was at all solemnized.

After the wedding, Emilie bore a girl, Subhash Chandra Bose named her Anita. (Presently, Anita Bose is the Professor of Economics in Augsburg University, she is married to Prof. Martin, who is a honourable member of the Green Party in Germany's Parliament).

Few people knew about Subhash's marriage, even his family did not know about this; therefore, he wrote a letter to Sharat Chandra in 1943 in which he informed about his marriage. He wrote in this: "Emilie Bose is my wife and Anita Bose is my daughter. If something unfortunate occurs to me in the service of motherland, I entreat you to look after them. I assign you this responsibility."

Later, Sharat Chandra Bose visited Vienna to see Emilie, and requested her to accompany him to India; however, Emilie decided to live there itself with the memories of her husband alive in her heart, and she continued to live there itself.

European Experience

During his sojourn in Europe, Subhash visited a number of countries; he met philosophers, thinkers and politicians; but it was not a purpose of tourism; rather, he wanted to understand the political background of those countries as well as their opinion about India. He wanted to clarify the sacred goal of the Indian struggle, which had been depicted in a deformed way by England. He also studied history, revolutionary movements and government and non-government organisations of those countries, so that they could be adopted in India if needed. Wherever he visited, he examined the Constitutions there, and accumulated technical knowledge related to national consciousness.

Impressed by Rome, he had written: "India needs a party which is focussed for India's freedom, as well as is able to draft the country's Constitution and implement the plan for national reconstruction. Therefore, we should be ready for two plans simultaneously – military organisation for attainment of freedom and reconstitution of the country after freedom."

Subhash learnt the policy of neutrality at international level from Turkey. The Turkey's ruler had adapted his country into a modern structure with the advice of foreign advisors. It had adopted the policy of neutrality, so that no other country could interfere in its internal matters. In this connection, Subhash wrote: "After freedom, India's foreign policy will follow the principle of neutrality or non-alignment. It will not interfere in mutual differences of European countries."

He also studied the detective system in Ireland. In his view, the detective movement of Sin Fen was an ideal for India's freedom.

In this way, the experiences accumulated by Subhash Chandra Bose in Europe were all aimed at India's freedom and the later Indian system. He tried to gather as much information as could be possible, so that he could draw from it for national development.

Instruction to Congress

In the year 1935, the Congress was celebrating its silver jubilee. On this occasion, Subhash Chandra Bose instructed the Congress thus: "India earnestly hoped that a peaceful pact could be signed through *Satyagraha*; it was thought that through non-violent struggle, India would be able to bring to a halt the entire country's administrative system as well as awaken the consciousness of the British people outside the country; however, all such hopes were belied. The *Satyagraha* movement has succeeded in creating an uproar in the country, but it has not much impacted the government, which has continued to be run on the old lines. Having failed to achieve its goal, the Congress is honestly looking into its heart. A part of the Congress has entered the legislative assemblies to advance towards constitutional activism. A faction, disappointed from the Congress, has constituted the Congress Socialist Party. The Congress ought to get sympathy at the international level together with its bid for opposition in India. For this, it should set up a foreign department, which could provide suitable information about India in international forums."

Subhash Chandra Bose, through his speeches and articles, was revealing to the world India's actual condition, so that the international community could have sympathy for the Indian cause of freedom struggle. A well-known writer and philosopher wrote about his efforts in this regard thus: "He has limitless love for the motherland and indomitable desire for freedom. He favours organised protest in place of terrorism, which does not exclude violence. Perhaps Bose has reached the limit of communism, so he has chosen the path of revolution in place of *Satyagraha*."

□

28
Return to India

For many days, Subhash was restless to return to the native land. Every now and then, he dreamt of terrorized sounds of the hapless Indian people. Mother India was calling her separated son ardently. He had been in Europe for close to three years. During this, he had done commendable tasks at the international level. However, now the desire to join the Indian freedom struggle was motivating him. He wanted to return to India and struggle with the British face-to-face.

Subhash was restless on one hand, and on the other, the countrymen were feeling the vacuum due to his absence; so Jawaharlal Nehru sent him an invitation to join the Congress Session at Lucknow. It pleased Subhash greatly. Until now he had checked himself from returning somehow, but now he found it impossible to hold himself back; he announced his return now.

His well-wishers tried to tell that the government could arrest him as soon as he reached India; moreover, the Congress had looked away from its Civil Disobedience Movement; it was not protesting against even anti-people ordinances. In such a case, his going to jail would become meaningless; so he was advised to work for the same goal from abroad. Moreover, he was not keeping good health, and any aggravation in it could further jeopardize the matter.

However, Subhash did not heed to this type of advice. He packed his luggage and headed for his country.

Subhash's Message

As was feared, as soon as Subhash reached Bombay on 8 April, 1936, he was taken under arrest under the government orders. This time, he was lodged in Yarvada Jail. This deprived him of attending the Lucknow Session. However, he managed to send across a message to Jawaharlal Nehru. It had just one sentence: "Keep the flag of freedom unfurled."

Despite being in jail, Subhash was speaking for the country's freedom. Just one-sentence-message from him inspired the people present in the session. With members' concurrence, Pt. Nehru sent a letter of sympathy declaring him a member of the Congress Working Committee. In it, he also assured him that the Congress would do everything possible to secure his release.

Government's Accusation

The Congress, under the leadership of Jawaharlal Nehru, demanded for the release of Subhash Chandra Bose; however, the then home secretary described the government's action as justified.

He accused Subhash thus: "We have examined all records about Mr. Bose right since 1924, and we have come to the conclusion that he aided in the revolutionary conspiracy. If he were freed, he would prove to be harmful for the country; especially because he is the master of extraordinary organisational prowess. In 1923, he had published an article in which he had asked the youths to sacrifice their lives. Subhash Chandra Bose is in direct personal contact with the terrorists, and he knows about the conspiracies to murder the government officials. He propagates communism. At Lahore Session of the Congress, he had urged to set up a parallel government. He also led the Yugantar Party, which was involved in attacking Chatgaon armoury as well as inciting other rebellions. We are certain that this man is related to the terrorists. We are confident that his definite plan comprises violent rebellion. If a promising man like him, with astute organisational capability to execute his ideas, is set free by the government, it would be a criminal stupidity."

In response, the Congress argued: "If the government possessed enough evidence against him, it could have moved against him in the court. The government states that his release would jeopardize the lives of those who are police informers, then we counter argue that it is better to risk their lives than deprive a man of his freedom, because depriving him from serving the country is worse than even death."

Arguments and counter arguments were given, but the government remained unmoved in its decision.

Subhash Day

It was thought that the government would not accept his release in a peaceful manner; so Nehru started the movement. 10 May, 1936 was declared as Subhash Day and a strike was urged. The entire country came to a halt. People took to streets to get Subhash released. Slogans rent the air, protests took place at every other place. Soon, this amber turned into a rising flame; in ten days, people's anger expanded into a countrywide movement.

The government was unnerved at this; but it did not want to be seen infirm, so it released him from jail and took him under house arrest at Sharat Chandra's house.

Still the movement went on, and Subhash's illness took an ugly turn. Compelled by this, the desperate government released him on 17 March, 1937, this time without any prior conditions. This news was published in the newspapers prominently. The entire country was elated. The movement had proved successful; now Subhash was free to serve the motherland.

On 6 April, 1937, Subhash was publicly facilitated at Shraddhanand Park in Calcutta. When he appeared in the assembly after a gap of ten months, the entire arena was filled with the sound of claps, thousands of hands went up in the air in his honour. Over six hundred offered him garlands and wished for his longevity.

On this occasion, Rabindranath Tagore sent him a message: "Together with the entire country, I too welcome Netaji Subhash Chandra Bose."

An Indian Pilgrim

Subhash was under treatment in Calcutta. After this, he was under treatment of Dr. Dharamveer at Dalhousie, but his illness did not improve. Finally, he proceeded to Austria on 18 November, 1937 for treatment. After his operation, when his health improved, he wrote a new book.

The book *An Indian Pilgrim*, was based on his life. He described a number of incidents of his life in a very interesting manner. He was as it is inclined towards writing; he finished this book in just ten days. During this period, Emilie was all along with him.

Victory in Britain

After recovering from illness, Subhash Chandra Bose went to Britain. There, he met the English politicians, philosophers

and thinkers. He grew so popular that he was felicitated at a number of places there. He was also given a dinner in his honour, in which British politicians joined. Newspapers carried articles praising him.

On 11 January, 1938, *Manchester Guardian* wrote: "Even those Englishmen who met him for the first time were favourably impressed by the mirthful and quiet nature with definitive ideas on Indian problems. He was now recognized as an international leader. Like Gandhi and Nehru, he too was like the Pole Star on the Indian political horizon."

During his visit to Britain, he was informed that he had been nominated by the Congress as the President for Haripur Session. He grew sentimental. Reacting to it, he said: "We will have to accept that we will have to bring India out to the world, on a wider scale than we have been doing until now. The problems of India are not confined to India alone; they are all related to the world. India is in contact with all progressive movements being run in other countries. Not only India's but also the world's well-being lies in them."

Finally, he was about to be crowned with the honour which he deserved so well. The time for the session was not far, so he concluded his visit in Britain and returned to India on 24 January.

□

29
President of Congress

Haripur was a small village in the district of Surat in Gujarat. It had been selected as the venue for the 51st Session of the Congress. The session was the responsibility of Sardar Vallabhbhai Patel. Hectic preparations were being made. The venue was named as Vitthal Nagar to bestow honour to Vitthalbhai Patel. A total of 51 gates had been erected in the town. The arena decorated with 51 gates looked like a royal court.

On the historical day of 19 February, 1938, Subhash reached Bardoli from Calcutta. He was magnificently welcomed at the railway station. People thronged the station in thousands to encourage and welcome their leader. He was mounted in a car decorated with flowers and taken to Haripur. The people in villages on the way supported him; they waived to him and hailed him.

At Haripur, he was seated on a massive chariot; this chariot, replete with floral decoration, was being drawn by fifty-one white oxen.

The procession went on for two and a half mile. Passing from the decorative gates, he accepted people's welcome. This grand welcome was not only for the Congress President, but also for a Yogi who had sacrificed everything of his own for the sake of country and humanity. Brimmed with motivation and spirit of service, this great leader was moved by his love for his motherland.

At this time, the future scene of India became clear in his mind. He wanted to lay the foundation of India on harmony, integration and cooperation.

Brilliant Speech

When Subhash Chandra Bose ascended the stage, he was elated in glory, his steps were like lightning. Today, he had the chance to address the nation, he had to stitch together the ideals and principles in order to present them as the goal. People had gathered in thousands to listen to the every word that would flow from his tongue. It was an important moment of his life.

He began his speech by striking hard at the British empire. He said: "A nation is formed, it develops and then it declines. Great Britain has already passed through the first two stages by now, it would not transform into an autonomous commonwealth of nations, like other empires, its decline is certain. Britain is living by making other countries its slaves; these slave countries are now ready to strike at the roots of its imperialist rule. There is no country in the world that is as proficient as Britain in executing the policy of divide and rule; it has been implementing this policy in India very heartlessly. In the new Constitution (Government of India Act, 1935), that the government has presented, it has described its intentions. If the country does not approve of the new Constitution, it would make the rights transfer as meaningless through its divisive policies; however, we should not understand that our methodology would remain confined to only constitutionality. There is enough time for this possibility. If the federal structure is forced upon our country, we will have to undertake even a stronger Civil Disobedience Movement. The Congress is in power in only seven provinces. It will have to augment its numbers and power. It is feared that taking over the power could result into a vicious outcome, so we have to guard against it."

Subhash also mentioned the problems of population expansion as well as other problems confronting the country. Expressing his views about solution of these problems and development of India, he said: "The country inflicted with poverty, starvation and disease cannot afford to increase its population; therefore, it ought to be our moral responsibility to check population. Poverty can be alleviated through the abolition of *Zamindari* system as well as complete land management. We will have to adopt scientific means for increase in agricultural production. There is abundant demand for crafts, cottage industry and handicrafts etc. We will require funds for promotion of agriculture, crafts and social system. It can be collected from India and abroad. The success of national project can be assured through equipment, which lack in India, so it is essential that a well-planned and systematic project is chalked out for scientific development of India."

'India is a multilingual nation. There are numerous languages, castes, communities and faiths here,' thinking this, Subhash Chandra Bose laid emphasis on national integration and unity. He also proposed to determine the national language as well as national script. Expressing his views about the national language, he said: "Both Hindi and Urdu are spoken in India. Therefore, the masses should use a combined form of these popular languages, that is 'Hindustani' should get the status of the national language."

Speaking about the national script, he said: "From scientific and historical viewpoint, no script has any role to play in faith or purity; regional languages have their respective scripts. Prevalent Hindu and Urdu are used in the scripts desired by people. From scientific and neutral viewpoint, I think that the problem can be resolved through the use of Roman script. Earlier I thought that a foreign script is anti-national, but when I went to Turkey, I experienced that it is the most advantageous to adopt a script which is very commonly prevalent. This script has the potential to bring India at par with other nations. As far as teaching it to the common people is concerned, ninety per cent population of India is illiterate; they will learn whatever script is taught to them. Besides, the knowledge of Roman script will help to learn European languages rather easily."

Speaking about the relationship of India with Britain, he said: "We have no personal enmity with the British government. We are struggling for our freedom. We will have complete freedom to decide upon our future relations. Why can we not establish friendly relations with Britain as a free nation?"

In the end, he discussed the prevalent condition of the Congress and said: "Some friends in the Congress think that the Congress should be dissolved after independence. This is a misleading notion, because the party which would beget the country freedom, would have to implement the work of its reconstruction too; it would have to bear the burden of administration. If the Congress is forcibly ended, it would end continuity. After freedom, the Congress will have to play three types of roles: to prepare the country for relinquishing selfish interests; to make efforts for India's unity and national integration; and accord provincial and cultural rights."

At the end of his address, the entire atmosphere rent with the sound of clapping, and Subhash Chandra Bose was given a standing ovation.

National Planning Committee

Subhash Chandra Bose favoured industrialisation. He was of the opinion that the Congress did not hold a uniform view on this, but at the same time, he admitted that the young generation was in favoure of industrialisation due to a number

of causes. According to him, it could solve the problem of unemployment as well as starvation by increasing agricultural produce. He had said: "To encourage industrialisation, much of manpower will have to be transferred, but the foundation of the new socialist party should be based on industrialisation. It is essential to compete with foreign industries; this will help the country progress of its own."

After Subhash became the President, he convened a meeting of provincial Congress committees and consulted them about improvement of economy according to the concepts of industrialisation. Then on 19 December, 1938, he constituted the National Planning Committee, and Jawaharlal Nehru was appointed its Chairman.

In this way, the credit for setting up the National Planning Committee goes to Subhash Chandra Bose.

Conflict of Ideas

Fire and water cannot sustain together, this adage came true so far as Subhash and Gandhiji were concerned. The moderate Gandhiji was the follower of non-violence. He believed in protest through *Satyagraha*, fasting and peaceful meetings. On the other hand, Subhash could sacrifice his life for the country's freedom even. Though he was not against Gandhiji's policies, yet he never supported him openly. He had his own ideals, his own policies, his own plans to execute the movement. He did not give importance to terrorism, but in his view, armed revolution was not improper either to gain freedom. He infused vitality in the youths in order to struggle against the British government. He said: "If the government does not consent by entreaty, it should be hurt so that it could realize the Indians' strength. It should know well that Indians were capable of giving messages of harmony, peace and love, but will not retract their steps if it comes to sacrificing their lives either."

Towards the end of the year 1938, the threat of the Second World War, was quite realistic. Subhash wanted to take advantage of these circumstances; he wanted to warn the British government that it should free India else armed rebellion would be conducted. However, Gandhiji did not agree with him.

According to him, this was in violation of the Congress's idealistic policy of non-violence. It was owing to his opposition that this resolution was dropped.

In this way, two diverse ideologies were at work simultaneously. Soon, the ideas conflicted, due to which the gap between Subhash and Gandhiji widened.

□

30

Gandhi-Bose Conflict

The Congress held its annual session in Tripura in December 1938. Looking at his popularity and people's trust in him, Subhash Chandra Bose decided to contest the election of the President once again; but Gandhiji, the axis of Congress, opposed him. He proposed the name of Nehru. As he had been on this post thrice, he turned down this proposal. After this, Gandhiji nominated Maulana Abul Kalam Azad. He reasoned behind this decision thus: "This step is being taken to cultivate trust in the Muslim community." However, Maulana expressed his inability due to ill-health. Finally, Dr. Pattabhi Sitaramaiya was nominated as a candidate.

Sitaramaiya was supported by Sardar Vallabhbhai Patel, Rajendra Prasad, Jairam Das, J.B. Kripalani, Daulatram, Jamnalal Bajaj, Shankardev Rao and Bhulabhai Desai, all stalwart members of the Congress Working Committee. They issued a statement saying: "The President of the Congress, by convention, has been appointed unopposed. It is only under exceptional circumstances that a person is allowed to contest elections for this post who had earlier been the President. Keeping these facts in view, Mr. Subhash Chandra Bose should withdraw his nomination from the path of Mr. Pattabhi Sitaramaiya."

This statement had been issued by the Working Committee, while other provincial Congress committees had supported Subhash. Now Subhash could see through the Congress's politics. He refused to withdraw his name. Arguing in his favour, he said: "This is no personal matter. Our struggle against imperialism has given forth new thinking, new ideas, new ideals, new programmes and new problems. People think that the election of the Congress President should be held above narrow considerations and programmes; it should be based on people's wishes and expectations. As far as I am concerned, I have no idea of any rule by which an individual cannot contest this election twice. If we glance at the history of the Congress, we find that it has been the case on a number of occasions. As it is, the election for the Congress President is held unopposed. Several provinces have nominated me without my knowledge. They urge that I should continue on this post. Indian masses too favour this. I haven't got even a single proposal which goes against this. If a devoted person like Acharya Narendradev is ready to assume the command of the Congress, I would delightfully take back my name, else the matter would be decided in the meeting on 29 January."

When the revolt was sounded, the Congress suffered upheaval; however, the Gandhiji's opposition could assure Subhash's defeat.

Gandhiji's Defeat

Gandhiji and other stalwart members of the Congress Working Committee were in the favour of Sitaramaiya; while Subhash Chandra Bose was ready to face all of them alone, like Abhimanyu. The national party of the country had been divided into two factions against each other. This was the struggle for truth, in which self-respect was at stake; it was like the Mahabharata of the modern times, in which Subhash was to break through the stratagem of politics, and he readied himself for this.

On 29 January, 1939, the result was declared. As against the hopes of the Congress leaders, Subhash Chandra Bose defeated Dr. Sitaramaiya by more than two hundred votes; Sitaramaiya was defeated despite Gandhiji's support; it stunned the entire country. Subhash had achieved his goal.

Until now, no one had the courage to challenge Gandhiji; so he grew desperate and said: "Dr. Sitaramaiya's defeat, in fact, is my own defeat." With this, he also gave signals to retire from the Congress. On his advice, the members of the Congress Working Committee too handed over their resignations.

Effort for Resolution

Subhash was agitated at Gandhiji's behaviour. Just then, he issued a statement and said: "Now my sole goal is to win over Gandhiji's trust. If I have won others' trust but fail to win the trust of Gandhiji, it would be quite an unfortunate thing for me."

Working in this direction, he tried to settle differences with Gandhiji. He urged him to secure to him the cooperation of the senior members, but Gandhiji remained firm; he expressed his inability and suggested to form a new working committee.

It was obvious that he did not favour any compromise; therefore, a disappointed Subhash returned.

Address to Nation

The Congress Session at Tripura was held on 10 March, 1939. About two lakh people were present to listen to Subhash; however, he could not attend it owing to ill-health. In his absence, his photograph was placed on the seat for the President, and the session was run by Maulana Abul Kalam Azad, while Sharat Chandra read out his presidential address.

"My countrymen, my friends, my comrades! You have elected me to the post of the President of the Indian National Congress, and have shown a great honour for me. The hearty and vigorous welcome that you have accorded me here in Tripura, I express my gratitude for this. This is true that you have given up certain formalities which are often conducted on such occasions; still I feel that your welcome has not been short in harmony and warmth. I hope that nobody will feel sorry for some shortcomings."

"My countrymen, now the time has come when we should raise the issue of Swaraj, and should put forward our demand to the British government as a warning."

"It makes me sad that there are some pessimistic people in the Congress who think that the time to end British imperialism has not come yet; but I don't see any basis for this pessimism when I look at it through a realistic viewpoint. As the Congress is in power in eight provinces, the power and prestige of our national organisation has shot up. The mass movement has progressed much in the whole of British India; Indian principalities too have awakened to the cause like never before. When else will it be a more suitable time to go for the ultimate struggle for attainment of freedom, especially at an hour when the international situation is in our favour? Speaking from harsh realistic viewpoint, I can claim that the present times are in our favour; therefore, we should firm up our optimistic sense. If we are able to forget mutual differences, if we are able to accumulate all our resources, if we are able to come together for national struggle, we will make it impossible for the British government to suppress us any more. Now what we have to see is whether we will rise to the occasion to take advantage of these favourable circumstances through political foresight, or miss this opportunity, which remains the most unique moment in our national life."

"We can see that the supreme power of the country is busy conspiring with the most of the principalities; would it not be proper for all Congressmen to approach the people in these principalities?"

"The Congress Working Committee should lead a popular movement at a large scale for creating a proper basis to attain civil rights and responsible governments in principalities."

"Comrades, today the atmosphere within the Congress is clouded; many differences have risen; therefore, many of our friends are disappointed and despaired; these clouds that you can see are all a fleeting phenomenon; and I can claim definitely that we will overcome the present difficulties and establish unity in the party. Vande Mataram!"

Resignation from Post

The meeting of the Working Committee was convened in March itself. Despite his illness, Subhash attended it. During this meeting, Govind Bhallabh Pant moved a resolution expressing trust in the old Working Commission because they had been selected according to Gandhiji's instructions. The resolution was passed with a majority, comprising even those members who had voted for Subhash for the post of the President. In fact, they had been perturbed following Gandhiji's opposition and clues of his retirement from politics, and this was the reason that they had supported the resolution.

Subhash was stunned by the wily tricks of politics. All his rights had been taken away despite the fact of his being the President. This injustice compelled him to think over; it was no more acceptable to him to remain on the post despite this dishonour, so he decided to resign.

Submitting his resignation in Calcutta Session on 29 April, 1939, he said: "In my view, I would have to confront great many problems in chairing the new Working Committee and it might have to elect a new President. Therefore, after due consideration, I resign; I have submitted this resignation with all cooperation in my mind; and I am hopeful that my resignation would serve the national interests. An atmosphere of non-cooperation has been created due to my becoming the President, and when all efforts to compromise did not bear fruit, this remained the only alternative to preserve my self-respect, prestige and duty towards the nation."

The Congress approved of his resignation immediately.

Reactions

The nation had been stupefied by the Congress conspiracy. The daily newspaper *Aaj* remarked: "Our respectable and old leaders should have acted with liberality. The exalted place that Gandhiji holds in the nation's heart; he could have preserved his prestige; the so-called liberal people of the party could have listened to their hearts; regrettably they did not do this; and the outcome is nothing but unfortunate, as well as harmful for old leaders and Gandhiji."

Another newspaper wrote: "The Congress has taken advantage of its glory in order to remove a challenger to the leadership by trickery. Subhash Chandra Bose is not an evil person, nor does he desire any post; his highest wish is to make the Congress take an early decision in the favour of movement."

Writing about Gandhi-Bose controversy, a prominent daily wrote: "Subhash Chandra Bose wanted to strengthen the Congress in order to enable it to struggle with the British, while the Gandhist leaders were hoping for an agreement with the government, they were displeased with him. In 1938 and later, Subhash Chandra Bose set up the National Planning Committee for a large scale industrialisation and its implementation at the national level. It annoyed Gandhiji all the more because he was against industrialisation. After the Munich Act of September 1938, Bose had started to prepare the Indians for the national movement through open propaganda, so that it could become a contemporary of the forthcoming war in Europe. All people liked this plan, but the Gandhists disfavoured it. They did not want any obstacle in their ministerial posts and parliamentary work. They were against starting the national struggle at that time, the consequence of which Subhash Chandra Bose had to bear with."

The national poet, Rabindranath Tagore too was hurt by this incident. He honoured Subhash by a long article titled *Deshnayak*. He also wrote letters to Gandhiji and Nehru for a compromise.

However, the situation remained unchanged; the conflict had taken deep roots.

□

31
Forward Bloc

Now the Congress supporters felt that Subhash, after his quitting the President post, would become helpless, disappointed and alone. They considered that his political career was as good as finished; however, Subhash Chandra Bose was cast from a different type of fabric that could be torn away by opposition. He stood firm like a rock, it was impossible for him to retract from his goal; and he went on to prove this within three days.

On 3 May, 1939, Subhash announced the founding of a new organisation called Forward Bloc, a faction with the Congress. Stating its goal, he said: "The constitution of the Forward Bloc has been undertaken to infuse a new vitality in the working of the Congress. Its goal is to unite the leftist forces within the Congress and give momentum to the freedom movement. As soon as the circumstances are favourable, it would initiate a campaign for complete Swaraj."

The All India Conference of Forward Bloc

was held in Bombay on 22 June 1939. Addressing it, Subhash said: "We should keep politics aloof from religion completely, because religion is a personal feeling. The working method of this party is not limited to only freedom struggle, but also post-war reconstruction. Its goals would comprise guidance, control and development of the principalities. It will have to assume the national responsibility through principalities. This plan will not waver owing to any emergency. If leaders are not properly trained in reconstruction, India will be a victim of disorder. Training of new generation will not be over and the responsibility of leaders will not be over until the young people are able to assume leadership of the country. The first stage of the Indian revolt will comprise of national movement against Britain, and the second stage will be struggle against inter-party conflicts. In that state of the struggle, all rights, distinctions and selfish interests will have to be eradicated in order to establish complete social, economic and political equality."

Besides the above, the party's Constitution was prepared and the following resolutions were passed:

- Not to allow the religion to rule the roost over political matters.
- To staunchly oppose regionalism.
- To end corruption spreading in the Congress due to desire for power.
- To emancipate the Congress from vested interests and make it lively and dynamic.

After the conference, Subhash set out on a nationwide tour in order to energise the Forward Bloc.

Autocratic Order

A few days after the session of the Forward Bloc, the Congress Session was held. In it, two resolutions were passed in the absence of leftists. It angered Subhash, and he announced to observe Protest Day on 9 July, 1939.

The Congress warned him, but he did not care for it and led the protest march on the specified day; on his exhortation, demonstrations, processions and public meetings were held all over the country.

This only agitated the Congress Working Committee. On its behalf, Gandhiji drafted a resolution, and then the same day, an autocratic order was issued. According to it, the Congress Working Committee was not in conformity with the rebellious actions of Subhash Chandra Bose. The party considers his actions as violation of party discipline; and on this basis, he is suspended from the Congress party. For three years, he would neither be an elected member of the Congress, nor would he chair Bengal Provincial Committee.

Subhash had expected such step, he had prepared himself for this in advance; he accepted this order.

Forward Bloc Paper

After his suspension, Subhash busied himself with the work in the Forward Bloc. He also started a weekly called *Forward Bloc*, through which he criticized the Congress policies as well as the wicked activities of the government.

By now, the Second World War had commenced. England issued a special ordinance to declare India a party to it. For this, no consent was sought from the Indian leaders, nor were they informed about the actual situation. Subhash advised the Congress to take advantage of the situation and start a nationwide movement; however, the Congress did not heed to his advice and supported the government.

Agitated by this, Subhash wrote in the editorial of the *Forward Bloc*: "Today India demands an assurance from the Congress Working Committee in clear terms that it will not compromise with imperialism. Can the Congress give this assurance? The people who think that the Congress is anti-agreement, I would like to tell them something. When the war was started, Gandhiji, without the consent of the Congress Working Committee, went to Shimla and assured the Viceroy that he was ready to cooperate with Britain in the war without any preconditions. You might know that the Congress has been delaying the demand for complete Swaraj ever since the war has started, and now the demand for the Constituent Assembly has been raised. What type of attitude has Gandhiji adopted about the agreement for the last six months? A sorry chapter is about to end in India, and preparations are underway to initiate a new era. The dark black night of oppressive imperialism is about to end, and with this will start a new dawn of freedom, democracy, socialism. If we wish, we can accept the heritage. Therefore, if the Congress Working Committee does not come true to our norms, it becomes our duty that we come forward to create a management system which can take over the responsibility of fighting a long war against British imperialism."

Siraj-ud-Daula Day

Subhash decided to observe Siraj-ud-Daula Day on 3 July, 1940 in the honour of the last Ruler of Bengal. The same day, he had plans to destroy Calcutta's Hallwell Memorial, which was about 150 years old and a symbol of India's slavery, as the first step in the movement.

Subhash wanted to destroy the memorial himself together with his volunteers. However, just a day before on 2 July, he was taken under arrest under Section 129 of the Indian Safety Act.

Life at Stake

In the beginning, Subhash was charged under life imprisonment section, but when he was elected as member of the central legislative council. His sentence had been suspended, and the trial was being conducted at a slow pace. Four months passed this way. Protesting this lax attitude of the government, he announced fast unto death on 29 November 1940.

He appealed to the countrymen saying: "I do not want to live any more under the present circumstances. I cannot bow before the British government, which is bent upon injustice and improbity, and I cannot assassinate my principles and ideals. If the administration can keep me arrested on the basis of unlawful power, then I too have every right to destroy this life protesting against its unethical practices. The world is mortal and nothing is eternal; however, ideas, ideals and dreams can never be destroyed. In my view, a martyr's sacrifice never goes waste. Freedom is not a crown of flowers, its achievement requires to

suffer from troubles, calamities and sacrifices. I opine that nothing has been realized in the world without hard work and penance; no dream can be realized otherwise. I am confident that my life's sacrifice will illuminate the path of cutting away the shackles of slavery."

"My countrymen, never forget that the greatest bane is slavery; bowing before injustice and improbity is the greatest sin. Now when the end of life is certain, why should it not be better sacrificed for the country? Remember, if freedom can be realized at the cost of life, it is still cheap."

Subhash's health was going down owing to fasting and illness. His aggravating condition scared the government. Therefore, he was released from jail on 5 December, 1940 and was lodged in house arrest at his residence.

Clandestine Plan

Subhash was deep in thought during his house arrest. He had vowed for service to the nation; he was dedicated to this cause; he had suffered numerous troubles for this; he had underwent expulsion; he had been in jail; but he was not sorry about all these; rather he thought that these were the happiest days of his life. The British government had failed to harm him, but he had been hurt by his own people. The very Congress for which he had spent invaluable moments of his life, had broken his trust. He wanted to sacrifice everything of his for the country; he had the courage to bleed for the motherland; he could get his head severed for the sake of freedom; but selfish people had isolated him.

He was thinking on these lines, when his mind was flashed with the words of Savarkar. A few days before, he had said to him: "A courageous and enterprising young man should set out of India and assist the enemies of Britain to throw out the English rulers through armed invasion."

'Yes, this is the thing I'll do. I'll go abroad and will gather a military force. I'll undertake armed rebellion for the country, for countrymen and for freedom of the motherland,' he resolved within him.

In association with five reliable comrades of Forward Bloc – his old comrade Niranjan Singh, Jamshedpur's trader Sardar Baldev Singh, member of Kirti Kissan Party Sardar Achchhar Singh, Comrade Ramkishan and Comrade Bhagatram – he made a secret plan to escape.

Now he was awaiting an appropriate moment.

□

32

Escape from Country

The government was keeping a close watch on Subhash Chandra Bose. His house was surrounded by detectives who were informing the government everything about him. About sixty-five policemen were deployed on the watch. Subhash was permitted to walk only up to the boundary, and not beyond. He was prohibited from meeting any outside person, nor could he write any letters. All that was brought into the house was searched well, but Subhash little cared about all this. He now closed himself in his room; he grew his mustaches and beard; he appeared to be some sage now. His room had the pictures of Vivekananda and Ramakrishna Paramhansa on the walls. The whole day he lay on his bed in deep thoughts. He had holy texts like the *Geeta* and *Ramayana* near him; he did not allow anyone to enter his room; he took

food only through the window. All this secrecy kept everybody in dark about the event that was about to unfold in near future.

See you again!

January 1941. The watch was showing the time of twenty-five past one o'clock; the date 17 January had changed into 18 January; people were all sleeping in their cosy beds; but on that dark night, a house on Algin Road had traces of a slight movement. This house belonged to Subhash Chandra Bose, today he wanted to execute his plan.

Wearing Aligarh trousers and black shervani (long coat), with black cap on the head and round specs on the eyes, Subhash walked out of the room softly. He crossed the gallery and reached the backyard. He did not allow anybody to know about his movement. He opened the door that opened in the street without a sound, then he peeked out to judge everything outside. When he saw the entire environment enveloped in complete silence, he stepped out and without a sound, walked towards the other edge of the street.

The street opened on a wide road, where a car stood. Subhash opened its door swiftly and entered the back seat. The car driver was Shishir, his nephew, younger son of Sharat Chandra. He glanced back for a while, and then started the engine and drove ahead speedily.

Leaving the town of Calcutta behind, the car was running at its full speed on the deserted road. Soon, it crossed the town limits. To allay any doubts, Subhash had adorned the dress of a Maulvi; his future plans were forming in his mind. He closed his eyes and sunk in thoughts. Shishir kept his attention on the road. He wanted to deliver his Kaka at some safe place.

With the morning hours, the car entered Dhanbad. There, Subhash Chandra stayed at the residence of his elder brother, Ashoknath Bose. He kept his garb on so that the servants would not doubt him, and then on the night of 18 January, he made to Gamoh, from where he took Delhi-Kalka Mail.

During the journey, a Sikh co-traveller asked him his name; he told him that he was Maulvi Ziauddin. On the way, Akbar Shah, a leader of Forward Bloc met him. Their glances met and then he sat a little away. Everything was going as per the plan, Subhash was completely satisfied.

Both of them stood up when the cantonment station approached and climbed down. Outside, a comrade was ready with a *tonga*. Subhash took it to Tajmahal Hotel in Peshawar. There a room was already booked for him. The same evening, he met Bhagatram, he was a reliable man. His entire family was connected with patriots and revolutionaries. As Subhash did not know a word of Pashto, he was advised to act deaf and dumb, so that the British agents could not identify him.

Now, Bhagatram was responsible to take Subhash Chandra from Peshawar to Afghanistan.

The next day, before Subhash set out on his journey, he daubed the mother earth on his head; it was not acceptable to him to quit the motherland in this manner, but he suppressed his emotions, still his eyes streamed down with warm tears. A sentimental Subhash addressed his motherland: "Maa, I migrate today for your freedom; I shall return soon to get you free from the shackles of bondage. Forgive this son of yours, O mother, until then. See you again…!"

With this, he proceeded towards his destination with Bhagatram.

Uproar in Country

The plan had so cleverly been executed that nobody could come to know of his flight. Only ten days later on 26 January, his family members informed about his absence. His house at Algin Road sank in grief; the news that spread around was about his absence.

The government was astounded. The English officers were out of their wits thinking how he could slip away despite such a strict watch, but they could have any clue of his flight. Orders were passed and policemen spread across the length and breadth of the town to sniff him out, all paths leading out of the town were blocked; detectives were employed to bring out some news about him, but all this effort proved futile. They little realized that the bird had flown over the country's borders.

Gandhiji was amazed. He telegraphed to Sharat Chandra to know the reality. In response, he said: "We are as ignorant of Subhash's plan and destination as is the public. We don't know even the time of his departure. Despite all endeavours over the past three days, we have not been able to get any clue. The situation points to his *Sanyas* (renunciation of the world)."

This incident was covered by a prominent newspaper of the country thus: "The watchmen kept watching the cage and the bird flew away. It is only Subhash Chandra Bose who can trick the British government; he alone can challenge the death. In this way, he has proved that the government cannot defeat him despite its thousand eyes. It depends on his sweet will what, when and which work he will do. The government can neither obstruct him, nor can impede his path. Subhash is a lion who has warned the oppressors in the jungle of imperialism. His flight will certainly commence a new chapter in India's history."

Assurance of Germany

Suffering difficulties and facing dangers, Subhash Chandra Bose and Bhagatram finally reached Kabul, the capital of Afghanistan. He took refuge at the house of Uttamchand Malhotra, a former member of the Naujawan Bharat Sabha. He tried to contact the Russian Trade Agency to set out of Kabul. He kept going round the trade agency for three days, he even tried to stop the ambassador's car to talk to him, but to no avail.

Looking at listless response from the British embassy, Subhash knocked at German embassy.

He marched into the embassy confidently and told the German ambassador everything, and sought his assistance in getting out of Afghanistan. He said to the ambassador: "If Germany gets ready to help, I can assure that it would not be a difficult task for us to defeat Britain."

The German ambassador assured him: "Mr. Bose, we'll cooperate with you fully; but you will have to wait until we get instructions from the German government."

Thus, the matter was postponed for a few days.

Flight to Berlin

On one hand Subhash had met the German ambassador; and on the other, Bhagatram contacted the Italian embassy through his contacts. Those days, Italy and Germany were working in close cooperation. The Italian ambassador displayed interest and formulated a plan to take him out with the help of Germany. Subhash was to be sent to Germany on an Italian passport, so his photograph was sent to Italian embassy. In a few days, a passport was readied for him; he was named Count Orlando Mazzotta in it.

On 18 March, 1941, Subhash Chandra Bose entered the Russian borders by car with an Italian and two German associates. And on 28 March, 1941, he took an aeroplane to Berlin from Moscow.

On 3 April, 1941, this brave son of India reached Germany from India.

□

33
Bose's Diplomacy

Three powerful countries – Germany, Italy and Japan – had, during the Second World War, formed an alliance called Axis Powers. They were also assisted by Hungary, Bulgaria and Romania. These nations were against England in the war, so Subhash Chandra Bose was interested in enhancing ties with these nations. He was confident that he could get India freed with their assistance.

He reached Germany anyhow. Now he was trying to draw their support in the favour of India. Thinking this, he sent a confidential letter to the German government.

Referring to the wilful policies of England, he wrote in it: "Despite assurance during the First World War, Britain has continued to occupy India. In the present war, it seeks to augment its power through Indian resources, so that it could challenge the New Order a few years later. India wishes to see Britain defeated with an aim to achieve freedom. The Indians are full of enmity and rebellious spirit at this time. Therefore, they can cooperate in practical terms with other powers in rooting out Britain. If the Indians are assured that the victory to the Axis Powers would help India gain freedom, then we would have to focus our attention to Europe, Afghanistan, India and India's border areas with the help of India and Axis Powers. For this, a provisional government will be formed at Berlin. Also, the Azad Hind Radio Station will be founded to announce the commencement of revolution in India, and arrangements will be made for broadcast from it. India should see the light of freedom with the victory of Axis Powers, and then the free Indian government and Axis Powers will enter into treaties. The Axis Powers will help India financially, and the free Indian government will be under obligation to repay this accepting it as a debt."

However, the letter was not replied to.

On 9 April again, Subhash wrote a letter mentioning five important points:

- Announcement of freedom for India and Arabian countries.
- Arrangements for revolt in these countries against Britain.
- Invasion of British government by Axis Powers.
- To obstruct the working of Britain-supported Afghanistan government for invasion of British India.
- If need be, to assist Iraq for war against Britain.

Speaking about its advantages, Subhash Chandra Bose stated that it would create, on one hand, a long series of friendly nations of Germany right from north Africa to far-east Japan; and on the other, if Germany enters into conflict with Soviet Russia or Turkey in the future, it would have the sympathy of continental countries.

This trick worked. Hitler considered his letter seriously. He knew that he was a popular leader in India and could, given a chance, announce revolution against Britain; it would make the war against Britain rather easy. Therefore, he consulted Mussolini and then he accepted the conditions put forward by Subhash Chandra Bose.

Azad Hind Legion

The German government soon arranged for financial aid, radio broadcast and military training to the Indians living in Germany. His office was made in Berlin itself. Adam von Trott zu Solz was aiding him on behalf of the German government.

Expressing his respect for Mahatma Gandhi, Subhash Chandra Bose set up the Azad Hind Legion on 2 October, 1941, which comprised 3,000 Indian troops taken prisoners of war. On this occasion, he invited the immigrant Indians living in Germany.

Addressing them, Subhash said: "Today I stand remote from mother India, in German capital Berlin, but I don't feel that I am far from my motherland. The warmth you have displayed has only encouraged and firmed up my will power. From today, we will together execute a plan by which we can free our motherland and put it on the path to prosperity. Today on the pious occasion of our great and respectable leader Mahatma Gandhi's birthday, we gather here to take a vow that we will not rest until we have freed our loving motherland from the foreign shackles. The German government has given its hearty support and assured cooperation. From today, we will work for the victory of our lovely country India. Therefore, the only term that we will use for wishing one another and as war cry will be Jai Hind. Jai Hind! Let us all vow that we will sacrifice ourselves for the country."

The Azad Hind Legion started with thirty-five comrades, most of them were students; however, this number swelled gradually. C.N. Nambiar, a journalist in Europe for past eighteen years and Ganpule, former member of Bombay Congress, joined it as members. Later, they both proved to be reliable comrades of Subhash Chandra Bose.

Structure of the Legion

The first meeting of the legion was held on 2 November, 1941. In it, the new members were initiated and given oath to patriotism. Besides, four important resolutions were passed:

- Subhash Chandra was acknowledged as the only leader of India and was given the title of Netaji. (It was after this he became famous as Netaji Subhash Chandra Bose. This title has become part and parcel of his identity so well, that this very word brings the image of Subhash Chandra Bose to the mind).

- Free Indian union was given the slogan of Jai Hind, which became popular in south-east Asia and became an identity for the Azad Hind Fauz. (Even today this remains on every child's tongue).
- The song by Rabindranath Tagore '*Jana Gana Mana*', was recognized as the national anthem. (This has been continued by the Government of India after freedom).
- The mixed form of Hindi and Urdu, Hindustani language was recognized as the national language of free India, and the Roman script was made the national script.

In the pattern of the Tricolour, Subhash Chandra Bose had made a springing lion as the symbol of free India. This was how the provisional government came into being. The main functions of the legion were to collect propaganda material for the Azad Hind Radio, publish and distribute *Azad Hind* newspaper, take care of Indian immigrants in Germany, and maintain other branches of the legion.

Writing about the influence of Subhash Chandra Bose on the legion, a German officer wrote: "Mr. Bose was the nerve centre of all tasks in the legion. He was a powerful leader and able chairman. His analysis was constructive and his mind was always filled with new ideas. He did not pay attention to his private tasks. His heart was filled with liberality. It was his influence that all members, despite their difference of opinions, had taken the common goal of freedom of the motherland."

Azad Hind Radio

Subhash Chandra Bose was demanding of the German government for radio broadcast. Speaking in its favour, he argued: "Propaganda for revolution should begin with radio broadcasts, so that the Indian masses don't have to depend on the British radio to know the occurrences and circumstances. This can help to raise revolt against the British government for freedom."

After a long dialogue, Germany accepted his proposal. The agreement provided that Azad Hind Radio would be an autonomous institution and its secret broadcast would concern only British government in India. The government had promised that it would not censor the talks relayed by the members of the legion.

In November 1941, Azad Hind Radio broadcasts began with ten efficient people. The legion was given a powerful transmitter, installed at a secret place, which could be accessed only by a few people. The work of the radio station was to gather news stories and reports, and translate them into different regional Indian languages according to Indian audience. This broadcast was started in three languages and its duration was forty-five minutes.

Azad Hind Fauz

The Indian troops who were fighting from the British side, taken prisoners of war, were brought to Berlin. Subhash Chandra Bose wanted to form an Indian national army. He appealed to the German government to hand over the Indian troops taken prisoner. This appeal was accepted.

On the advice of Subhash, Nambiar went to prisons in order to bring about a change of heart of the Indian troops. This effort bore fruit in no time; and a massive army of the union was made. This force came to be known as Azad Hind Fauz.

□

34
Historical Speech

Japan defeated the British forces and occupied Singapore. Taking advantage of this, Subhash Chandra Bose addressed the country on Azad Hind Radio. It was his first speech after his flight from India.

Welcoming the countrymen, he said: "I, Subhash Chandra Bose, am addressed to you directly through Azad Hind Radio. I have been awaiting silently and patiently for the incidents to unfold for the past one year, and now the time has come, so I am talking to you. Standing at the crossroads of world history, I declare on behalf of India and all freedom-lover immigrant Indians outside India that we will continue to fight against British imperialism continuously, until India becomes the master of its own fate. During the period of the movement and during the period of reconstruction of India, we will cooperate with those who will help us drive away the enemy. The fall of Singapore is the beginning of the fall of the British empire. This is a beginning of the new era. Britain has enslaved us and has destroyed our morality and economy fully. God has presented the auspicious time to free India; in this age, there is no greater enemy of freedom and progress than Britain. After my flight from India, the British government has been issuing misleading and contradictory details about my activities. In these calamitous times, the British government would have found infinite joy in seeing me dead, but fate had something else in store. Comrades, our countrymen are no more required to bow before the British any more, because now the prestige and glory of the country rest on our shoulders. The struggle that I have started, I am hopeful that I'll get your complete cooperation. United we can destroy the British empire. I exhort you all Indians to unite and join the struggle for freedom together. Jai Hind!"

The news of Subhash's being alive elated the Indian people, while the British government was unnerved. Friendship of Subhash with enemies created a tumult in England too.

Impression on Hitler

The Axis Powers had not declared their future post-war policy concerning freedom of India. Though Mussolini had agreed to make this declaration on 5 May, 1942 and Japan too had agreed, but Germany maintained its silence in its regard. Subhash was curious to know its viewpoint, so he decided to meet Hitler. After untiring efforts, on 29 May, 1942, Adolf Hitler, the dictator and most dangerous person in the world, and Subhash Chandra Bose met.

Hitler shook hands with Subhash Chandra Bose to welcome him and addressed him as Netaji for the first time.

In his autobiography, commenting on India, Hitler wrote: "The Indians' efforts to free themselves from British shackles are not likely to materialize. India can hope to be free only when Britain is defeated by a more powerful military power. A nation, that is weak in political and military power, cannot overcome a politically and militarily stronger power. It is better to allow India to reel under Britain rather than help an uncivilized and uncontrollable India."

During their meeting, Subhash objected to this statement and asked Hitler for an explanation, but Hitler refused to comment on it.

The next question Subhash put was: "Will the German government declare freedom for India after the war?"

Hitler was silent for some time, and then he remarked, "India cannot be able to rule itself for another one hundred and fifty years."

After a while, Hitler stood near the world map and said in clear terms: "The German border war is so far from Indian borders; therefore, there cannot be any practical advantage of any immediate declaration of independence of India."

Subhash was astonished at this. Hitler had indirectly refused to extend any help.

Just then, Hitler asked him: "What steps will you take for India's freedom struggle when the circumstances are so adverse?"

At this, Subhash could no more remain patient, he said in English to the officer standing there: "Please tell him that I have spent all my life in politics. In this connection, I don't need anybody's approval."

This was how the meeting ended in disappointment and failure. However, Hitler was greatly impressed by Subhash's personality. As a result of this, he removed the objectionable comment from his autobiography. Later, he helped Subhash to transport him to Japan.

Invitation to Bose

Rashbehari Bose was a well-known Indian revolutionary. He had migrated to Japan in 1912, and had provided momentum to the Indian freedom struggle there. Inspired by Subhash Chandra Bose, he too founded the Azad Hind Legion there. In one of its conferences, he had passed a resolution to form a national army for India. Under it, those Indians were recruited in it who had been taken prisoner by the Japanese during the war. Following the footsteps of Subhash, he too named this army as Azad Hind Fauz. The Japanese government was assisting it in every way. Rashbehari wanted that Subhash should lead this army, so he invited him to Japan.

Germany had indirectly refused to assist. Moreover, its position in the war was gradually weakening too. Therefore, Subhash found no other way but to agree to go to Japan. He wanted to take the Azad Hind Fauz with him, but it was no easy task to ship so many troops. So, the German government said in clear terms that one person could be sent with him, and no other. At this, Subhash decided to take with him Abid Hassan, an engineering student, who was his private secretary too. As it was not possible to go by air, arrangements were made to ship him across.

Berlin to Tokyo

On 8 February, 1943, Subhash Chandra Bose, accompanied with Abid Hassan, travelled by train to Keel, from where they took a German submarine U-190. Only very close people knew of his voyage. His tapes were recorded so that no one could know about his departure from Germany.

The submarine travelled along the English Channel and along West Africa in the Atlantic Ocean, and crossed the Indian Ocean on 29 April, 1943. There, a Japanese submarine was awaiting him. He was shifted by a rubber boat to the other submarine.

Subhash reached his destination on 6 May, 1943. High-post officers of Japan welcomed him. Five days later he reached Tokyo finally on 16 May.

The journey from Berlin to Tokyo was extremely risky, but Subhash faced this risk with a smile on his lips.

□

35

Japan's Support

A formal meeting was held between Prime Minister General Hideki Tojo and Subhash Chandra Bose on 10 June, 1943. Only twenty minutes were prescribed for the meeting, but Tojo was so impressed by Subhash's personality that their meeting lasted four hours. Until then, the Japanese looked down upon Indians, but his attitude towards India was transformed after this meeting. In this connection, Tojo had said to his advisor: "This Indian is great, no doubt there can be a no other more competent fellow to lead the Azad Hind Fauz."

On the government invitation, Subhash attended the Japanese Parliament on 16 June, 1943. There in the assembly of Japanese ministers, he delivered his historic speech, in which he expressed his anguish over British brutal policy and sympathy for India's freedom struggle. Besides, the ministers promised Subhash all possible help for attaining freedom.

In this way, Subhash was able to obtain Japan's support. Now, he did not need to hide himself.

On 19 June, 1943, he convened a press conference and issued a statement. In it, he said: "In the First World War, the

British politicians tricked the Indian leaders. Twenty years ago itself we had decided that we would not become the victim of this foolery any more. In all these twenty years, all Indians have been struggling for freedom. We were waiting for an opportune moment, and now that moment has finally arrived. India got nothing from Britain but spiritual decline, cultural disintegration, terrible poverty and political slavery; so, we all Indians are ready with our courage to break away all British chains and get freedom. The Axis Powers are all ready to assist us to declare war on our eternal enemy; however, we will flow our blood to attain freedom, because freedom can be preserved only through sacrifice and hard work. If the enemy fights with a sword, we have to reply with a sword only. The non-violent struggle will have to be changed into an armed struggle. If Indians are able to pass through this test, they are sure to win, and in reward, they will kiss freedom."

This statement created upheaval in the world. Burma admired him for this and sent him an assurance saying that it would render all possible help to realize the national glory and freedom.

Commander-in-Chief

Subhash stayed in Tokyo for forty days, and then he left for Singapore. There, the Azad Hind Legion, immigrant Indians' nationalist party and Japanese army command welcomed him under the leadership of Rashbehari Bose.

On 14 July, 1943, a mass meeting was held. Addressing it, Rashbehari Bose said: "Now you have before you none else but Subhash Chandra Bose, there is no need to give his introduction. He is the true son of Mother India and a warrior. Today, in your presence, I resign from my post and propose the name of the patriot Subhash Chandra Bose as the President of the Azad Hind Legion of east Asia. Also, I declare him as the Commander-in-Chief of the Azad Hind Fauz."

Addressing the gathering, Subhash Chandra Bose said: "Any agreement with the British government would be harmful for us and our interests. We have to be ready for renunciation and activity. Depending on non-violence and civil disobedience principles. This struggle has reached the transition stage. The goal and objective of our new organisation will be to carry out armed struggle against British imperialism. Those who have any doubts should trust me. I shall remain loyal only towards India. I am living for India and will embrace death for it. I am planning to form a provisional government of free India, so that we can unite all different ingredients to strengthen ourselves. The goal of the provisional government is to make the Indian revolution successful. The task of the provisional government will end after the British empire has been abolished. After this, the Indian people will be able to form their own government."

He was supported by an uproar of loud claps.

March to Delhi

On 5 July, 1943, Subhash formally announced the constitution of the Azad Hind Fauz. It was the first occasion when he was in full military dress. Taking salute of thirteen thousand troops, he addressed them in a glorious voice.

In his speech he said: "It is a glorious day of my life today. God has bestowed infinite honour and privilege on me that I might announce the coming of Azad Hind Fauz into existence. This army will not only get India rid of British shackles, but also will create national consciousness of a free India."

"When in 1939, Germany attacked France, the German soldiers had only one slogan on their lips: 'March to Paris, March to Paris.' Now, the slogan for us is, 'March to Delhi! March to Delhi!' We tie the coffin to our heads and light a flame of patriotism in our hearts with a resolve to conquer Delhi."

"No one knows who will survive and who will not in this struggle, but I am sure know that victory will be ours ultimately. Our task will not be over until our surviving warriors march over the graves of British empire to the Red Fort in Delhi."

"We have to strengthen the foundation of our national security so strong that we might not have to lose our freedom ever again. For this, we will have to bear such patriots in every home, in every family who will not be scared of sacrificing their lives."

"In the present situation, I can give you nothing but hunger, thirst, penury and death, but if you stand by me in life and death, then I am confident that I will deliver you to victory and freedom. It is not important who of us will live to see India free. It is enough that India is freed. We will devote everything for attaining our freedom."

"You are the preserver of Indian national honour and concrete form of India's hopes and aspirations. Your conduct should be such that the countrymen bless you, that the future generations should take pride in you."

"I assure you that I will be with you in every situation – dark or light, pleasure or sorrow, trouble or victory. Jai Hind!"

Rani Jhansi Regiment

Subhash wished that every section of the Indian community should take part in this struggle for freedom. In his opinion, there was no distinction between rich and poor, caste and creed, man and woman. He said that all sections could, at their own levels, do much. It would unite the society as well as augment the power to struggle. It was on this basis that he exhorted the brave women: "I don't want an incomplete, but a complete military organisation. If Hind's army comprises men, it should as well comprise women too, who should stand with their male counterparts on equal footing. Until they take up responsibility in the future, the Azad Hind Fauz remains incomplete. This struggle is as much theirs as ours; therefore, I urge all women to take up arms like the Rani of Jhansi and lead the freedom struggle. Their sacrifice for the country will be remembered for ages to come, I have no doubt about this."

The women were shaken out of their limitations. They were not yet aware of their energies and were watching the movement from a distance: However, then Subhash had shown them a new path, a new vista, motivated by which the Indian brave women united and announced the formation of the Rani Jhansi Regiment. Their enterprise inspired others too who so far had been mute spectators. They too determined to join the struggle with body, mind and wealth.

Reconstitution of Provisional Government

After Subhash Chandra Bose became the President of the provisional government of free India, he set down to reconstitute it. He delegated the power into different departments such as secretariat, propaganda, finance, accounts and audit, recruitment and training, woman hostel, transport, health and social welfare, education and culture, provincial department and foreign affairs minister. Different sections were set up in different departments on this basis. Emphasis was laid on mutual coordination and cooperation among different departments. All these departments were assigned the task to secure recruitment of more and more troops, to arrange for provisions and ammunitions, and collect grants for the economic system.

In this way, Subhash Chandra Bose was systematizing the government as a skilful leader.

Grievous News

Meanwhile, Subhash received the news of his mother's death. He was shocked for a while. He had as good as forgotten his mother. This grief brought tears to his eyes; but he was confident that his mother would forgive him for his neglect because he was fighting for the motherland, that was reeling under the imperial shackles, and that was looking up to Subhash for emancipation.

Freedom of the motherland will be the true tribute to her, Subhash said controlling himself.

□

36
Government of Free India

Burma was recognized as an independent country on 1 August, 1943. It invited Subhash as the special guest to its independence day celebrations. Addressing a meeting in Rangoon, Subhash said: "During its rule of India, the British government made a lot of promises to the Indians; these promises proved to be mere words on the paper; on the contrary, the promise given by the Japanese Prime Minister General Tojo has stuck to the promise during the war period that he made on behalf of his government and nation; this remains but true that Asia cannot be emancipated without the freedom of India, so Indians will have to present themselves for this task, so that the remaining countries too can become free."

On this occasion, he requested the Burmese government to set up a centre for the government of free India at Rangoon. His request was turned down owing to some reasons, but later, Burma acceded to this on the condition that the government of India will not interfere into its internal matters.

After this assurance, Subhash started making arrangements for the provisional government.

On 21 October, 1943, a large assembly was held at Singapore in which one thousand Indian delegates from east Asia took part. This session passed the resolution for the provisional government.

Subhash Chandra Bose was appointed its President unopposed. Taking oath he said: "I, Subhash Chandra Bose, in the name of God, solemnly swear to get India and its thirty-eight crore Indians free. I will keep fighting this battle for freedom to my last breath. I shall remain a servant of India and will protect the interests of my countrymen; this will be my supreme duty. I will be available at all times to preserve the freedom even later and will be ready to sacrifice even the last drop of my blood for its preservation."

In his statement, he also referred to the warriors of 1857 as well as Gandhiji's Non-cooperation and Civil Disobedience Movements. In this way, he was providing a momentum to the struggle in a planned manner.

Looking at the advancing steps of Subhash, India was elated with hopes. People were now confident that he would return to get the country free, and the British empire would crumble to dust.

Declaration

After his address, Subhash issued his declaration. In it, he discussed the importance and functions of the provisional government and said: "Our government is not a peacetime government; it is a struggle committee. The cabinet will comprise of a few civil officers, while some officers will look after the armed force. This is the final phase of the struggle. Now the Azad Hind Fauz will cross over the Indian boundaries and march towards Delhi, and this will be the beginning of the battle. This campaign will rest only after we defeat England and America and hoist the Indian Flag on Delhi's Viceroy House."

Before the statement was concluded, he laid emphasis on the goal and said: "It will be the responsibility of this government to attain the confidence of the Indian people, after the British empire has been crumbled, and form the new national government. The government of the Azad Hind Fauz will rule until the British are driven out of India. It promises every citizen's religious freedom, equal rights and equal opportunities. It also vows to maintain national prosperity and peace."

The declaration was signed by Subhash Chandra Bose as the Prime Minister, War Minister, Foreign Minister and Supreme Commander of the Azad Hind Fauz. A 21-member council of ministers was also declared which comprised five ministers, eight Azad Hind Fauz officers and eight Indian representatives living in south-east and east Asia. Rashbehari Bose became the principal advisor. The responsibility for the woman wing was given to Captain Lakshmi Swaminathan. The minister for publication and propaganda department was S.A. Ayyar while the minister for finance department was Col. A.C. Chatterjee. The legal advisor was A.N. Sarkar.

Declaration of War

Now, the provisional government of free India had been set up; about fifty thousand soldiers were now ready to sacrifice their lives for the motherland; financial constrains had been overcome, and now powerful countries of the world were with it.

After intense discussion over important factors, finally on 24 October, 1943, on radio from the headquarters of the government, Subhash Chandra Bose declared direct war against Britain and the United States.

Addressing the countrymen, he said: "Mother India has been crying under the shackles of imperialism; Britain has given her numerous wounds; our hearts were agitated; our souls were burdened by the mother's debt; our hands were eager to break away those shackles which were like a blot on our freedom; but we could do little but to see all these things. Weaknesses squeezed out our power, but today, we all stand under the same flag, now the time has come to confront the oppressive British. We affirm that we will continue to fight with the British troops until the last drop of our blood."

This declaration of war filled the Azad Hind Fauz with vitality. The motivated soldiers started to raise the war cry: "Jai Hind! Jai Subhash!"

International Support

After the declaration of the war, Subhash got busy with foreign tours with a purpose to secure support for the provisional government. At first, he attended the east Asian conference, organised in Tokyo. There, he was welcomed as the head of the state. In this session, Tojo, on behalf of Japan, declared to hand over Andaman and Nicobar islands to Subhash Chandra Bose. Also, he explained that Japan was not interested in expansion in India or deriving economic benefit out of it. The other countries present in the session expressed sympathy for the Indian freedom struggle and supported the resolution for support. On 10 November, 1943 the Japanese emperor met him and appreciated his efforts. It was a memorable day for Subhash.

After this, he visited Nanjing, Shanghai, Manila, Jakarta, Borneo, Sumatra and gathered support for his cause. In this tour, lasting five months, he not only estimated the circumstances in the favour of free India, but also accumulated financial aid from the migrant Indians.

Shaheed and Swaraj

Andaman and Nicobar are like places of pilgrim for the Indian freedom fighters. Andaman was the place where Indian patriots were kept imprisoned in the name of *Kala Pani*; it was well-known for the inhuman and unbearable oppressions by the British government. However, now this island group had fallen under Japan. After Japan handed over Andaman and Nicobar group of islands to the free Indian government, this became the first state of India to get free.

Subhash Chandra Bose set foot at Port Blair in Andaman on 10 November, 1943. It was for the first time that Subhash had touched the land of India after he had escaped from here. The same day, he visited the military headquarters in order to acquaint himself with the administrative set up. The next day, he hoisted the Tricolour and addressed a large gathering.

He said: "Occupation of Andaman signifies the first province of India taken free from the British snare. This is very important for us. This place has become a symbol of the British conspiracies and terrible tortures. Every particle here is permeated with the pitiful cries and screams of the revolutionaries. We will secure the freedom of the entire mainland India much like Andaman."

Renaming the islands, he said: "From today, Andaman will be called Shaheed Dweep (martyr island) and Nicobar will be called Swaraj Dweep (independence island). These will be like the symbols of Indian freedom struggle."

This was how Subhash unfurled the Indian Flag in Andaman and Nicobar and left for Singapore.

□

37
Freedom for Blood

"My friends! My warriors! Sons of Mother India! Rise and get ready for the struggle. Bound in the slavery shackles, Mother India is now calling for sacrifice of heads in its struggle for freedom. Daub your forehead with blood and take up the arms, and devote yourself at the feet of the Mother. Our fellow Indians are looking towards us with hopes and aspirations; rise and march on the path of freedom; the distance between us and our freedom is just this much. The auspicious day, that we were waiting upon, has finally dawned. Our arms are eager to drown the enemies in blood; our hands are eager to throw oppressors out of India. Therefore, take no more time and advance ahead.

"Never waver from offering your blood on this path. O warriors, I need your courage, I need your confidence, I need your heads, I need your blood. I want all that from you that you can sacrifice. I exhort you to give me blood, and in return I will give you freedom."

"Remember that the price of blood that flows for the sake of motherland will be freedom. Every drop of blood that flows from our body will write a tale of destruction of the imperialists. O fearless warriors of free India, take a vow that free India will be daubed with the enemies' blood. We shall sacrifice ourselves for the sake of our country and make the history of India glorified. Jai Hind!"

It was on 3 February, 1944 that Subhash Chandra Bose had addressed the Azad Hind Fauz in this manner; and on the very next day, that is 4 February, 1944, with the first rays of the sun, he issued the orders to attack British India.

The army was divided into four brigades – Gandhi brigade, Nehru brigade, Azad brigade and Subhash brigade. It was under the command of Shahnawaz Khan. As soon as the command was given, the army marched towards India.

The troops sang and marched:

"Kadam-kadam badhaye ja, khushi ke geet gaye ja,
Yeh zindagi hai qaum ki, tu qaum par lutaye ja."
(March step by step and sing the songs of elation;
This life is of the nation, sacrifice it for the nation).

The freedom enthusiasts were marching to meet the motherland singing and laughing. The obstacles they faced on the path appeared to them as delicate as flowers. They did not bend upon getting the country freed. Their footfall on the ground made a sound which resonated the entire environment. The rising dust storm from their feet was making a bid to drive away the British rule.

On 21 March, 1944 the Azad Hind Fauz set foot on the Indian soil. It was passionate scenery as the sons of the soil daubed the earth on their foreheads; they bowed to the sacred land. And then, they hoisted the Tricolour and sang the national anthem.

The same day, Subhash Chandra Bose convened a press conference at Rangoon headquarters and announced to the world: "The Azad Hind Fauz has entered India, and the battle for India's freedom is being fought on the Indian soil."

Influence of Hind

The Azad Hind Fauz attacked at the Indian borders ferociously. The British army confronted it. The Indian troops were not afraid of death, they had already decided to sacrifice themselves in the battle. Their only goal was to seek the country's freedom. Therefore, they advanced ahead and attacked the enemy. Their bravery and fighting skills took the British military officers by surprise.

Gradually, the British army found to be at the receiving end; its army started to retreat; soon, the Azad Hind Fauz succeeded to occupy Paletava and Daletame regions. A little away was the Modak post from where the British kept watch on the Indian borders. The Indians troops planned and attacked this post. The British army fled after some fighting, and with this, the Tricolour was hoisted there.

After this, the Japanese and British troops conducted a joint attack on Kohima. The British army was alert this time. It responded with a heavy bombing, and with it started a terrible battle. The Indian troops dared to confront the enemy, and in no time, the Indian soldiers overcame the opposition.

On 6 April, 1944 the Tricolour was hoisted at Kohima.

Subhash's Perception

Though Japan was cooperating in every way, but its attitude was now clear; it wanted to bring India under its control, as it had done with Burma previously. Subhash Chandra Bose did not trust it. Perceiving a threat, he appointed Col. A.C. Chatterjee as the governor of the freed areas. He wanted that the officials of the provisional government should enter India and assume the post of the provincial governor. He assigned Nambiar with the responsibility of passing legal ordinances, making appointments and other functions. He also set up a headquarter on the hills near Mandalay, where a large part of the interim government was transferred. From here, he guided the Azad Hind Fauz and started working on the constitution of the civil government. For finance, the Azad Hind Bank was opened and notes were printed.

In this way, Subhash Chandra Bose saved the Indian regions from falling under the Japanese influence.

Title of the Father of the Nation

Gandhiji and Bose possessed divergent opinions. They had diverse paths for the realization of freedom; but this too was equally true that Bose respected Gandhiji from the core of his heart. He said: "Gandhiji's policies in the capacity of a politician were lax and insufficient. His supremely contented nature is like a bane to the national interest, but as a person, there cannot be any slack for respect, honour or devotion to him. In the present times, he occupies the supreme place among the great people. This is the result of his morality and social service. He has transformed himself from an ordinary being to a great man."

When the Azad Hind Fauz was battling with the English forces on the Indian borders, Subhash Chandra Bose broadcast a message for Gandhiji on radio. He said: "I, Subhash Chandra Bose, respect the Father of the Nation Mahatma Gandhi. The entire country honours him; it follows his ideals and principles, therefore, I want to assure this honourable personality of the nation that the provisional government is working for the freedom of the country; it has no selfish motive behind it, nor has it a mentality like that of Britain. In fact, it is a part of India which will be assimilated into India after freedom. Trust me that our only goal is freedom of the country; we will not gain anything by opposition. You are like the Father of the Nation; therefore, O Father of the Nation, we need your cooperation and blessing for victory. Jai Hind!"

This was for the first time that Subhash Chandra Bose had addressed Gandhiji as the Father of the Nation. After this, this title became a part of Gandhiji's identity.

□

38
India's Defeat

On 23 January, 1945 Subhash celebrated his birthday with fanfare. On this occasion, the members of the government weighed him with money. He was seated on one side of the scale and on the other were offered rupees. People donated openheartedly. A trader called Habib donated one crore rupees. Besides, gold and silver jewellery too was offered. Women went to the extent of donating their *mangalsutras*, the mark of their husbands.

This money was to be utilized for acquiring rations and provisions for the Azad Hind Fauz as well as treating the wounded soldiers. So, all this money was handed over to the finance department.

The same day, news was received that the Japanese force had been defeated in the Irawati region.

Subhash went to that area immediately and motivated the troops of the Azad Hind Fauz saying: "This surrender has been done by the Japanese army; the Indian Army has not yet surrendered which is fighting for Indian freedom, because a true revolutionary never accepts defeat, he is never disappointed or discouraged."

He took over the command himself; just then he came to know that the infantry unit of the Azad Hind Fauz had dug in at a little distance. He wanted to inspect it himself, while that area was seized by the enemy from all around. Therefore, Shahnawaz Khan objected to it. He said: "You are growing selfish, you have no right to risk your life without any justifiable cause. Your life is the wealth of the country, I will not allow this invaluable treasure to be threatened."

In response, Subhash said: "You don't have to worry about me. Not yet a bomb or bullet has been cast in England which could assassinate me."

After this, he confronted the dangers and inspected the infantry unit.

Adverse Situation

The Azad Hind Fauz had been fighting for the past ten months. During this period, it occupied a number of British posts and lost many others; but every time, the troops fought with the British army with zeal. They cared for neither food, nor clothes, nor sleep, nor lack of provisions. Whenever they exhausted their ammunition, they grappled with the enemy troops with bare hands. This spirit of their patriotism took the world by surprise. However, there were people among these patriots who were about to lose their confidence, they were looking for an opportunity to get out of the skirmishes; the situation grew so hopeless that some people were ready to betray even. This betrayal harmed the Azad Hind Fauz significantly.

On the other hand, the Japanese army's attitude underwent a change. It was due to Subhash Chandra Bose, who had shut at their mouth any opportunity to benefit from the Indian situation. The Japanese army was responsible for supplying provisions and assisting in the war, but now Japan was not inclined to risk its troops without any tangible advantages. With this, the Japanese army began to retreat. Whenever fighting broke out, it put the Indian troops in the front. In the meanwhile, Japan was desperate following the American attacks on it, so all Japanese units fighting in India were called back; it contributed to weaken the Azad Hind Fauz.

Subhash tried to bring together the units fighting at different fronts, but the rain made the situation difficult for them. The military units could not keep contact with each other. It became impossible to supply them provisions and assistance.

Hunger and epidemic claimed many lives. Gradually, the situations grew adverse and its steps now wavered from going towards the goal.

Sting of Defeat

The Allied countries had crushed the Axis Powers badly. Japan had been rendered helpless when it was seized by America. Adolf Hitler had committed suicide in Germany. This victory filled a new vigour in Britain. Now, it faced the Azad Hind Fauz more resolutely.

The Azad Hind Fauz became helpless before the British forces owing to lack of arms, absence of air cover, falling number of troops and spreading epidemic. It could not bear with the determined attacks from the British army, and it had no other alternative but to retreat.

The Rani Jhansi Regiment was at the front, Subhash was responsible for its security. He confronted problems and tricked death to take it safely to Rangoon, and from there, he sent the troops away to Singapore by air.

Subhash wanted to command the Azad Hind Fauz in India, but his well-wishers advised him to leave Rangoon. After a long debate, he decided to leave for Singapore.

Before his departure from Burma on 24 April, 1945, Subhash addressed the officers and men of the Azad Hind Fauz and said: "I am going from Burma with a heavy heart. We have been defeated in the first phase of the freedom struggle, but many more phases have to come yet. Defeat in the first phase gives me no reason to feel desperate. The stories of your bravery in the plains of Imphal, hills and forests of Arakan and oil fields as well as other areas of Burma will remain unforgettable in the history of our freedom struggle. In this time of this calamity, my only command is that when you fall fighting, the Tricolour must still be in your hands. Die like a brave, so that the highest ideal of honour and discipline is maintained. With your renunciation and sacrifice, the future generation will not be born slave, it will be born free, and it will remember you in exalted terms. It will acclaim you because it is your struggle and temporary failure in Manipur, Assam and Burma which ultimately led to the illumination of the divine path."

"I have to leave Burma on the advice of my ministers and officials so that I can continue with my struggle for freedom. I assure you that our countrymen in east Asia and India will continue with their struggle; your suffering and renunciation will not go useless. As far as I am concerned, I will try to manage all possible resources for their freedom. In the end, I appeal to you to remain optimistic. It is always dark before the day dawns. India shall be free and it is not very distant. Jai Hind!"

With this, Subhash Chandra Bose departed from Burma with a sting of defeat.

Final Message

The Azad Hind Fauz had been surrounded from all sides; a number of its troops were killed in the war; those who dared not sacrifice themselves, offered themselves for surrender. The British government shot at or hanged some prisoners of war claiming them to be traitors. Some prisoners were brought to Delhi and lodged in the Red Fort. Everything had come to an end.

In 15 August, 1945, Subhash Chandra Bose addressed the troops for the last time and said: "In our bid to get India freed, we have been trapped in a disaster which we had not dreamt of. It might appear to you that you have failed in your mission for Indian freedom, but this failure is only temporary. Your past achievements cannot be destroyed by the defeat or shocks. It is your duty that you ought to continue to display your impregnable optimism and determination. There are many paths that lead to Delhi. Our destination is Delhi. No power on earth can keep us under bondage. India will be free soon, and then we will start a new era."

He delivered a message to the immigrant Indians of east Asia thus: "You have sacrificed lives and wealth for India's freedom, and this is proof enough of your patriotism and self-renunciation. I will never be able to forget your readiness and vigorous response when I urge you for military organisation.

You should continue to recruit your sons and daughters in the Azad Hind Fauz and Rani Jhansi Regiment. I regret still more than you that we have not immediately realized the fruit of your suffering and renunciation; however, this temporary failure should not disappoint you. Let not your trust in the future of the country waver even for a moment."

□

39
Ultimate Journey

Subhash Chandra Bose had never learnt to accept defeat. He had displayed on many occasions the wonderment of turning the most adverse conditions in his favour by his indomitable courage and intelligence. He was certainly disappointed by the failure that he met in the Indian freedom struggle, yet his vigour and belief in the realization of the goal was not yet shattered. He studied the contemporary situation. Japan had surrendered after America atom bombed Hiroshima and Nagasaki. The American forces could arrest him at any moment at the behest of Britain, so it was advisable for him to leave Singapore, but he was undecided about his destination; he was actively thinking about this.

Britain and America were not on good terms with the Soviet Union; a conflict was taking place between them. Subhash wanted to take advantage of this situation. In the past, during the Washington security conference, the Soviet Union had expressed its support for the Azad Hind Fauz indirectly. Therefore, Subhash was confident that the powerful Russia would help him in the Indian freedom struggle. After due consideration, he decided to leave for the Soviet Union.

Subhash expressed to the Japanese government his desire to go to Russia. He proposed that he could go alone if it was inconvenient to send all of them together and his ministers could be sent later.

The Japanese general headquarters disapproved his proposal, but the Field Marshal of Japan, Terouchi was impressed by Subhash Chandra Bose greatly, so he arranged for his departure on his own responsibility. At twenty past nine in the morning on 16 August, 1945, Subhash reached Singapore airport together with some of his comrades – Colonel Habiburrahman, S.A. Ayyar, Col. Pritam Singh and Mr. Nigeshi. It was a confidential movement, so only a few comrades were present there. Standing at the entrance of the aeroplane, Subhash waved his hands to his comrades and said: "The circumstances are adverse against us, but we will make them favourable. The goal of my journey to Russia is to reconstitute the Azad Hind Fauz. With their aid, we will compel the British to quit India; have courage until then. I assure you that India will surely get freedom. We shall live in a free India soon. I know there are many obstacles in its path, but our victory is definite under all circumstances."

The aeroplane took off at ten o'clock; soon it left Singapore behind; the very place which had been a witness to India's freedom struggle.

Three hours later, Subhash landed in Bangkok. He passed that night discussing with his comrades there. The next day morning, three more comrades joined him – Col. Gulzar Singh, Major Abid Hassan and Devnath Das. Prior to setting off, Subhash Chandra Bose hugged all his comrades and bid them farewell. His heart was heavy before leaving; his eyes became moist. Subhash controlled himself and went ahead. Only God knows why he felt this to be their ultimate meeting.

Farewell Friends!

Subhash and his comrades arrived at Saigon at ten o'clock in the morning. He held secret discussions with Japanese officials at the airport itself, in which he was assured of any further assistance. After this, Subhash took some rest at the residence of Narayan Das, the residential secretary of the Azad Hind Union. About two hours later, some Japanese officials arrived by car. They held their discussions in camera. At this time, Col. Habiburrahman was present in the chamber.

A few minutes later, Subhash walked out of the chamber with Habiburrahman, and went to the room where other comrades were staying. Subhash said to them: "An aeroplane is about to take off from Saigon in a little while. The Japanese officials have consented to accommodate only one of us in it. Now the point to decide about is if you will agree in case I have to go alone."

Everybody was stunned. They did not like to send him alone. Ayyar said: "Tell them forcefully that at least one more man should be accommodated in it."

The officials were approached once again, this time they agreed with this. Subhash decided to take Habiburrahman with him.

Soon all of them were at Saigon airport. Subhash bid his comrades farewell and ascended the staircase to reach at the main entrance of the aeroplane. Suddenly he turned and waiving his hand and said loudly: "Farewell, Friends! See you again. Jain Hind! Jai Bharat!"

With this, he went inside with Habiburrahman.

On 17 August, 1945, at quarter past five in the evening, the aeroplane took off for an unknown place. The remaining comrades kept seeing it flying away and disappearing in the sky.

Sad News

On 21 August, 1945, people were still busy with their morning chores. Delhi Radio was relaying religious songs. All of a sudden, the programme was interrupted for sad news. The news was: "On 18 August, 1945 at nine o'clock at night, Sri Subhash Chandra Bose has died in an air crash at Taihoku military airport."

This left people gaping for breath. Just a few days before, he had promised to get the nation free, how then could he leave us behind with shattered dreams of our independence? The news shocked everybody. Nobody could believe it. People contacted the office of the secretary for India, where this news was confirmed. The brave son of Mother India had departed for all times to come. This made the entire country drown in endless sorrow.

Truth of Accident

There were seven people in the aeroplane together with Subhash Chandra Bose; of them, only Col. Habiburrahman had succeeded to remain alive. Divulging the mystery, he described every moment.

The aeroplane took off from Saigon and landed at Tureen (Indo-China). It stayed there for the night there. Next day at five in the morning, it took off to reach Taihoku airport (Taiwan). It was refuelled there. It was there that Subhash and Habiburrahman took meals. About an hour later, they climbed up the aeroplane and took their seats.

The aeroplane took off again at thirty-five past two, and all of a sudden, there was a massive thunder. Habiburrahman felt as if the aeroplane was under the enemy fire; however, Subhash sensed some technical snag. Soon, his doubt transformed into confirmation. The aeroplane's engine had ceased working, only the starboard engine was working. The aeroplane came down rapidly; the pilot tried to control it somehow, but all his efforts proved futile.

When confronted with death, Habiburrahman perspired profusely, but Subhash kept sitting on his seat with a tranquil emotion. His face glowed in glory, it appeared as if he were sinking deep in meditation.

Dash! The aeroplane struck the ground with a loud thud, and caught a massive fire. There was complete darkness before the eyes for a few moments.

When Habiburrahman regained his consciousness, he looked around. Badly wounded Subhash stood near him, the remaining passengers had been killed. They came out of the burning aeroplane somehow. Subhash's clothes had caught fire as he was drenched in gasoline. He tried to open his coat belt; Habiburrahman helped him to extinguish the fire, but until then, most part of his face and body had been burnt; he had a one-inch-long wound on his head too.

He fell down unconscious.

In the meantime, assistance reached there. The wounded Subhash was taken to the military hospital, he was still speaking in that terrible situation: "Tell my countrymen that I fought until the last moment and I am sacrificing my life for their sake. No power can keep our country under bondage. They must keep struggling, our country will be free soon."

However, the fate had something else in store. The doctors could not save him despite all their efforts. On 18 August, 1945, this Son of Mother India closed his eyes forever. His last words were: "I want to have sound sleep."

Subhash is survived by millions of Indians, who were eagerly awaiting his return. They never knew that their deliverer had left for his heavenly abode.

Final Rites

The final rites for Subhash were conducted at Taihoku on 20 August, 1945. This moment was attended by Habiburrahman, Major Nagatomo, interpreter Nakamura, a Buddhist priest and manager for cremation.

His remains and ashes were preserved in a pitcher and preserved in an ancient Buddhist temple at Rankoji. It is in this temple that his death anniversary is observed every year on 18 August.

Mystery of Death

Col. Habiburrahman had confirmed the death of Subhash Chandra Bose, but as the dead body had not been found, a number of suspicions arose about his being alive. Some people opined that Subhash died while under arrest in Siberia, Soviet Union. On the contrary, some people refused to accept him as dead. They presented some impressive evidence in this regard too. Some people claimed to have seen him alive too.

After independence, at the entreaty of countrymen, the Government of India appointed a four-member committee under the Chairmanship of Shahnawaz Khan; it was assigned the task of discovering the truth about Subhash Chandra Bose's death. This committee also visited Japan in order to examine the circumstances. Those days, India did not have good diplomatic relations with Taiwan, so the government there did not assist in the matter.

After examination, the committee approved the statement by Habiburrahman.

However, the Indians could not accept this fact. They said that a great man like Subhash could not die so easily. They believed that he could be traced with the help of the Taiwanese government.

The Government of India constituted another committee under the Chairmanship of Justice Mukherjee. It examined the available evidence for six years from 1999 to 2005 and prepared a report in cooperation with the Taiwanese government.

This committee submitted its report on 8 November, 2005.

The Mukherjee Committee report submitted that, according to the Taiwanese government account, no such air crash had occurred at Taipei on 18 August, 1945 in which Subhash was travelling. Some information filtered in from American department which supported the Taiwanese account. The American sources revealed that no air crash had occurred during the said period. It is clear that Subhash did not die in the air crash. The remains kept at Rankoji temple in Japan, which is claimed to be Subhash's, is not his either.

The government dismissed the conclusions of the committee without assigning any reasons. It has also not made public many such documents which could resolve the mystery behind the disappearance of Subhash Chandra Bose. The reason was obvious, this could lead to souring of relations with some countries; therefore, the government was forced to dismiss the enquiry committee.

□

Timeline

1897	Born on Saturday the 23rd January at Cuttack in a Bengali family of lawyer Sri Jankinath Bose.
1902-08	Primary education in a missionary school meant for Europeans and Anglo-Indians. P.E. School.
1909	Joined Revenshaw Collegiate School, Cuttack. Learnt Bengali and Sanskrit. He developed hobby of Gardening.
1912	Received first political impetus after the visit of King George V.
1913	Stood second in merit in the whole of Bengal at matriculation examination. Errands to Haridwar and Banaras in pursuit of Yoga and religion. Lived in saffron dress. Aurobindo Ghosh became his ideal.
1914	Hunt for Guru at Banaras, Haridwar, Mathura, and Vrundawan proved fruitless. Rude and insulting behaviour of the British, bitter and frustrating experience at Presidency College, and outbreak of World War-I left a scar on his psyche.
1915	Passed intermediate examination in first division.
1916	Fir degree examination took Honors course in Philosophy.
1917	Owing to attack on Prof. Otten he was expelled from the University. Came back to home in Cuttack and devoted himself in social service tending patients in rural areas suffering from Cholera and small pox. Studied dream analysis, self-analysis, and practiced conquering and sublimation of sex instinct.
	Returned to Calcutta. Attempted to recruit in the 49th Bengal Regiment Rejected for bad eyesight.

Admission tried in Bangabhashi College but for want of Honours course joined third year in Scottish Church College. In rustication lost two years. Learnt Bible. Participated in Philosophical Society. Joined university unit of the Indian Territorial Army. First military training in life, and a year of soldiering.

1918 Engrossed in study.

1919 Passed B.A. Hons. Secured First Class and second in order of merit. Left M.A. course in psychology On 15th Sept sailed to England for ICS examination. Admitted I Cambridge I November. Subjects offered – Economics, Philosophy, Political Science, Geography with cartography, Sanskrit, English Composition, English History, Modern European History, and English law.

1920 In July appeared for ICS Examination. Stood fourth in merit in Sept.

1921 On 26th January wrote letter to father to give up Government service. Decided to devote life to Teaching and Journalism. On 28th April sent resignation of ICS.

1921-23 Political apprenticeship under C.R. Das. Became Principal of National College, Editor of National Newspaper 'Swaraj'. Became Executive Member of Bengal Provincial Congress Committee. Agitation against visit of Prince of Wales. Leader of Congress Volunteers Corpse. Civil disobedience. First gaol sentence. First political speech on ' Sincere work and patient suffering ' In charge of Food Relief Work. Worked as Secretary of Congress President C.R. Das. Formation of Swaraj Party of extremists.

1924 C.R. Das elected Mayor of Calcutta and S.C. Bose was elected as Chief Executive Officer of the corporation in October. Interned in Alipore jail on doubts of terrorism. Transferred to Great Fort of Mandalay in Burma. While in jail was nominated in January to the Bengal Legislative Assembly.

1926 Released from Burma. C.R. Das, his political Guru, was dead. Health deteriorated.

1927 He became natural leader of Bengal but in bad health. He refused to go to Switzerland directly from Burma. Elected as Chairman of the Bengal Provincial Congress Committee. Got busy in political reconstruction.

1929 Opposed Dominion Status.

1930 Entered full-scale civil disobedience. Arrested on his birth day 23rd Jan. for leading Independence procession. Sent for one year in jail. Went on hunger strike against shabby treatment by authorities. Released. Became Mayor of Calcutta on Sept. 25th. Became chairman of All India Trade Union Congress. (AITUC)

1938 Conferred with Gandhiji and reconciled. Accepted nomination as Congress President. Spent six weeks at Badgastein. Completed his half done autobiography 'An Indian Pilgrim' in ten days. Emilie Schenkl was his secretary. Visited England. Clement Attlee, Ernest Bevin, Sir Stafford Cripps welcomed him. Reception given at Dorchester. He met Zetland, Lord Halifax, George Lansbury, Harold Laski, Dr. Ivor Jennings, Prof. JBS Haldane Prof. GDH Cole, and Prof. Gilbert Murray of Oxford. Met Mussolini secretly On his birthday on 23rd Jan. reached Karachi. Presided over Haripura Congress Session at Vithal Nagar in Gujarath.

1939 Contested election for second time President of Congress against the wishes of Mahatma Gandhi and defeated his candidate Pattabhi Sitaramaiyya. Gandhi took it as his own defeat. He told all members of the CWC to resign. The Congress was on the verge of break-up and hence Bose resigned and formed extremists' 'Forward Block' within the Congress at Ramgarh. At the instance of Gandhi Bose was suspended from Congress for three years. As prophesised by him the Second World War began.

Gandhi wanted to help the British and Bose did not want to loose the golden opportunity to gain independence.

1940 Congress conference was at Ramgarh in Behar. Bose held 'Anti Compromise Conference' at the same time and the same place. Gave message to the nation to start struggle for independence without break. On July 2nd Bose was arrested for popular demonstration to remove Holwell Monument built in memory of victims (1857) of Black Hole. He was arrested under Defence of India Act. In jail he went on fast unto death on 29th November and after six days was released and interned in his house at Elgin Road , Calcutta.

1943 Visited Paris. Celebrated 26th January as Independence Day. On February 8th left by U boat-submarine from Keil for Japan. Only Abid Hasan accompanied him. On April 28th reached Indian Ocean and was transferred to Japanese Submarine Reached Sabang in Indonesia and then flew to Tokyo on 13th June. Gen. Tojo welcomed him on 13th June.

1944 On Jan. 7th Netaji shifted his H.Q. from Singapore to Rangoon. On 4th Feb. offensive in Arakan was launched. Formed Azad Hind Dal for Civil Administration of liberated territory. INA crossed the Indian border on March 19th. Imphal campaign was launched on 7th April. H.Q. was shifted to border near Mandalay. Imphal was captured on 21st April. The greatest mistake was not to capture Dimapur that was just forty miles from Kohima. Dimapur was last railway station and ammunition and food depot of the British. Due to internal conflict Gen. Sato wasted one month sitting idle on the hill looking over Kohima. Early onset of Monsoon disrupted the supply line. Starvation and death ruled INA. Retreat began and assembled in north Burma. Further retreat continued.

1945 In the consensus of scholarly opinion, Subhas Chandra Bose's death occurred from third-degree burns on 18 August 1945 after his overloaded Japanese plane crashed in Japanese-occupied Formosa (now Taiwan). However, many among his supporters, especially in Bengal, refused at the time, and have refused since, to believe either the fact or the circumstances of his death.Conspiracy theories appeared within hours of his death and have thereafter had a long shelf life, keeping alive various martial myths about Bose.

□□□